LECTIO DIVINA

OF THE

GOSPELS

FOR THE
LITURGICAL YEAR
2020-2021

UNITED STATES CONFERENCE OF
CATHOLIC BISHOPS

CONTENTS

Reading seeks for the sweetness of a blessed life,
meditation perceives it,
prayer asks for it,
contemplation tastes it.

Reading, as it were, puts food whole into the mouth,
meditation chews it and breaks it up,
prayer extracts its flavor,
contemplation is the sweetness itself
which gladdens and refreshes.

Reading works on the outside,
meditation on the pith,
prayer asks for what we long for,
contemplation gives us delight in the sweetness
which we have found.

— Guigo II, *The Ladder of Monks*, III (12th c.)

What Is *Lectio Divina* and How to Use This Book

Reading – Meditation – Prayer – Contemplation

Lectio divina or "divine reading" is a process of engaging with Christ, the Word of God. Through this sacred exercise, we enter into a closer relationship with the very Word himself, who communicates the love of the Father to us through the Holy Spirit.

Lectio divina has four steps in which we first hear what God has said (reading). We then take it in and reflect on it (meditation). From this our hearts are lifted up (prayer). Finally, after speaking to the Lord in prayer, we rest and listen for his message to us (contemplation).

This is the process of *lectio divina*. It is a conversation with God, grounded in God's own self-revelation to us. This helps us speak to God with a focus on what he has already told us about his relationship with humanity, his plans and desires for us, his promises, his admonitions, and his guidance on how we can live, so as to find true life in abundance in Christ.

Here is a brief description of each of the four steps:

Reading (*Lectio*)

Read the passage slowly and allow it to sink in.

If there is a passage that is particularly striking, and that you want to keep with you, consider committing it to memory, or writing it down to keep with you, so that you can re-read it throughout the day, and let it enter deeper into your spirit.

"Faith comes from what is heard, and what is heard comes through the word of Christ." (Romans 10:17)

"The word of God is living and effective, sharper than any two-edged sword, penetrating even between soul and spirit, joints and marrow, and able to discern reflections and thoughts of the heart." (Hebrews 4:12)

Meditation (*Meditatio*)

Read the passage again, and when something strikes you, a question arises in you, stop and meditate. Think about what God may be saying through it.

"It is the glory of God to conceal a matter,
and the glory of kings to fathom a matter."
(Proverbs 25:2)

"I will ponder your precepts and consider your paths." (Psalm 119:15)

Prayer (*Oratio*)

Speak to the Lord about what you have read and share what's on your mind and heart—offer and share with the Lord your thanksgiving, petition, concerns, doubts, or simply affirm, back to the Lord, the very word that he has spoken.

> *"Enter his gates with thanksgiving,*
> *his courts with praise."*
> *(Psalm 100:4)*

> *"Ask and it will be given to you; seek and you will find; knock and the door will be opened to you." (Matthew 7:7)*

Contemplation (*Contemplatio*)

This is a quiet time, a time to rest in his presence and wait upon the Lord. It is a time where we allow the Lord to speak directly to our spirit from within us. It requires practice. But this allows us to be attentive to the Lord's voice, and by regular practice, our ability to hear God's voice will grow in daily life and daily situations, as we learn to focus our minds and hearts, our thoughts, our concerns, and our hopes toward him.

> *"My sheep hear my voice; I know them, and they follow me."*
> *(John 10:27)*

> *"Be still and know that I am God!" (Psalm 46:11)*

Applying This Process of *Lectio Divina* to the Liturgical Year

This *Lectio Divina of the Gospels for the Liturgical Year* book will take the reader through the Sundays and major feasts and solemnities of the liturgical year. It can be used for individual devotion and can also easily be used to assist in small group reflections in parishes and small faith groups. It offers a structured process for engaging with the Word of God. As the reader or group becomes more comfortable engaging with Scripture, this process can be more closely tailored to suit the path of growth that best fits the reader(s).

First, the *lectio divina* session is started by praying a prayer that is taken from a Mass collect from that liturgical week. Following that prayer, the main scripture passage for reflection is read, which is taken from the gospel reading for that day. This READING can be re-read, a few times, to let it sink in. Next, a set of three questions are offered to help in MEDITATION. These questions can also facilitate talking about the passage in a group setting. The individual then offers his or her personal PRAYER, responding to the Lord. In a group setting, people can speak out their prayers one at a time—this may help deepen the prayer response and further set the group's focus on the Lord.

Next, a structured set of passages and questions are offered that return the reader back to the gospel passage. This invites the reader to contemplate what the Lord is speaking and what it means for their life. It allows the individual or the prayer group to consider specific ways the Lord may be speaking into their life at that very moment. As each person begins to hear a response from the Lord—the Lord's word spoken directly and personally to them—that person can begin let that word flow through their life, by an interior change and a will to do what the Lord is asking of them. Through this step of CONTEMPLATION, we hear God's voice speaking to us, and it propels us to conversion of heart and mind.

After the closing prayer, time is given to choosing how to live out the fruit of your prayer. You know your heart and life best—if it's clear what God is asking of you, in faith, choose some way that you can put that request or teaching from the Lord into action that week. It could be a small act of faith that the Lord is asking, or perhaps, a more serious and important step that he is asking you to take. If there is nothing specific that comes to your mind, consider the question and suggestion offered in the *Living the Word This Week* section. This portion offers guidance on what concrete actions may be taken in our daily lives.

The *Lectio Divina of the Gospels for the Liturgical Year* offers a specific pattern of prayerful reading of God's Word. As you begin on this path, may the Lord's blessing follow you, and fall upon you, throughout the movement of seasons in this new liturgical year, and may your life, in turn, be a blessing upon others.

LECTIO
DIVINA
OF THE
GOSPELS

November 29, 2020

Lectio Divina for the First Sunday of Advent

We begin our prayer:
In the name of the Father, and of the Son, and of the Holy Spirit. Amen.

Keep us alert, we pray, O Lord our God,
as we await the advent of Christ your Son,
so that, when he comes and knocks,
he may find us watchful in prayer
and exultant in his praise.
Who lives and reigns with you in the unity of the Holy Spirit,
one God, for ever and ever.

Collect, Monday of the First Week of Advent

Reading (*Lectio*)

Read the following Scripture two or three times.

Mark 13:33-37

Jesus said to his disciples: "Be watchful! Be alert! You do not know when the time will come. It is like a man traveling abroad. He leaves home and places his servants in charge, each with his own work, and orders the gatekeeper to be on the watch. Watch, therefore; you do not know when the Lord of the house is coming, whether in the evening, or at midnight, or at cockcrow, or in the morning. May he not come suddenly and find you sleeping. What I say to you, I say to all: 'Watch!'"

Meditation (*Meditatio*)

After the reading, take some time to reflect in silence on one or more of the following questions:

- What word or words in this passage caught your attention?
- What in this passage comforted you?
- What in this passage challenged you?

If practicing lectio divina *as a family or in a group, after the reflection time, invite the participants to share their responses.*

Prayer (*Oratio*)

Read the scripture passage one more time. Bring to the Lord the praise, petition, or thanksgiving that the Word inspires in you.

Contemplation (*Contemplatio*)

Read the Scripture again, followed by this reflection:

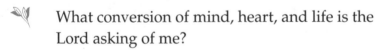 What conversion of mind, heart, and life is the Lord asking of me?

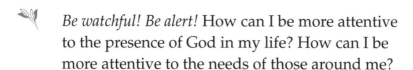 *Be watchful! Be alert!* How can I be more attentive to the presence of God in my life? How can I be more attentive to the needs of those around me?

You do not know when the time will come. How I am preparing to meet Christ when he comes again? Does the way I spend my time reflect the priority of Christ in my life?

May he not come suddenly and find you sleeping. What anesthetizes me to the demands that my faith makes on me? Do I give my faith my best energy and effort?

After a period of silent reflection and/or discussion, all recite the Lord's Prayer and the following:

Closing Prayer

O shepherd of Israel, hearken,
   from your throne upon the cherubim, shine forth.
Rouse your power,
   and come to save us.

Once again, O LORD of hosts,
   look down from heaven, and see;
take care of this vine,
   and protect what your right hand has planted
   the son of man whom you yourself made strong.

May your help be with the man of your right hand,
   with the son of man whom you yourself made strong.
Then we will no more withdraw from you;
   give us new life, and we will call upon your name.

From Psalm 80

Living the Word This Week

How can I make my life a gift for others in charity?

Carefully examine your schedule this week and judge whether it accurately reflects the priority that your faith should have in your life.

December 6, 2020

Lectio Divina for the Second Week of Advent

We begin our prayer:
In the name of the Father, and of the Son, and of the Holy Spirit. Amen.

Grant that your people, we pray, almighty God,
may be ever watchful
for the coming of your Only Begotten Son,
that, as the author of our salvation himself has taught us,
we may hasten, alert and with lighted lamps,
to meet him when he comes.
Who lives and reigns with you in the unity of the Holy Spirit,
one God, for ever and ever.

Collect, Friday of the Second Week of Advent

Reading (*Lectio*)

Read the following Scripture two or three times.

Mark 1:1-8

The beginning of the gospel of Jesus Christ the Son of God.

As it is written in Isaiah the prophet:

Behold, I am sending my messenger ahead of you;
he will prepare your way.

A voice of one crying out in the desert:
    "Prepare the way of the Lord,
make straight his paths."

John the Baptist appeared in the desert proclaiming a baptism of repentance for the forgiveness of sins. People of the whole Judean countryside and all the inhabitants of Jerusalem were going out to him and were being baptized by him in the Jordan River as they acknowledged their sins.

John was clothed in camel's hair, with a leather belt around his waist. He fed on locusts and wild honey. And this is what he proclaimed: "One mightier than I is coming after me. I am not worthy to stoop and loosen the thongs of his sandals. I have baptized you with water; he will baptize you with the Holy Spirit."

Meditation (*Meditatio*)

After the reading, take some time to reflect in silence on one or more of the following questions:

- What word or words in this passage caught your attention?
- What in this passage comforted you?
- What in this passage challenged you?

If practicing lectio divina *as a family or in a group, after the reflection time, invite the participants to share their responses.*

Prayer (*Oratio*)

Read the scripture passage one more time. Bring to the Lord the praise, petition, or thanksgiving that the Word inspires in you.

Contemplation (*Contemplatio*)

Read the Scripture again, followed by this reflection:

 What conversion of mind, heart, and life is the Lord asking of me?

 Prepare the way of the Lord. How am I preparing my heart for the coming of Christ at Christmas? How can I help bring the Lord to the people that I meet?

 Make straight his paths. What things block my path for following Christ? How have I been an obstacle in others' paths?

[People] were being baptized by him in the Jordan River as they acknowledged their sins. What sins go unacknowledged in my life? How can I avoid the sins that take me away from God?

After a period of silent reflection and/or discussion, all recite the Lord's Prayer and the following:

Closing Prayer

I will hear what God proclaims;
> the LORD—for he proclaims peace to his people.
Near indeed is his salvation to those who fear him,
> glory dwelling in our land.

Kindness and truth shall meet;
> justice and peace shall kiss.
Truth shall spring out of the earth,
> and justice shall look down from heaven.

The LORD himself will give his benefits;
> our land shall yield its increase.
Justice shall walk before him,
> and prepare the way of his steps.

From Psalm 85

Living the Word This Week

How can I make my life a gift for others in charity?

Make plans to receive the Sacrament of Penance before Christmas.

December 8, 2020

Lectio Divina for the Solemnity of the
Immaculate Conception

We begin our prayer:
In the name of the Father, and of the Son, and of the Holy
Spirit. Amen.

O God, who by the Immaculate Conception of the
    Blessed Virgin
prepared a worthy dwelling for your Son,
grant, we pray,
that, as you preserved her from every stain
by virtue of the Death of your Son, which you foresaw,
so, through her intercession,
we, too, may be cleansed and admitted to your presence.
Through our Lord Jesus Christ, your Son,
who lives and reigns with you in the unity of the Holy Spirit,
one God, for ever and ever.

Collect, Solemnity of the Immaculate Conception

Reading (*Lectio*)

Read the following Scripture two or three times.

Luke 1:26-38

The angel Gabriel was sent from God to a town of
Galilee called Nazareth, to a virgin betrothed to
a man named Joseph, of the house of David, and the

virgin's name was Mary. And coming to her, he said, "Hail, full of grace! The Lord is with you." But she was greatly troubled at what was said and pondered what sort of greeting this might be. Then the angel said to her, "Do not be afraid, Mary, for you have found favor with God. Behold, you will conceive in your womb and bear a son, and you shall name him Jesus. He will be great and will be called Son of the Most High, and the Lord God will give him the throne of David his father, and he will rule over the house of Jacob forever, and of his Kingdom there will be no end." But Mary said to the angel, "How can this be, since I have no relations with a man?" And the angel said to her in reply, "The Holy Spirit will come upon you, and the power of the Most High will overshadow you. Therefore the child to be born will be called holy, the Son of God. And behold, Elizabeth, your relative, has also conceived a son in her old age, and this is the sixth month for her who was called barren; for nothing will be impossible for God." Mary said, "Behold, I am the handmaid of the Lord. May it be done to me according to your word." Then the angel departed from her.

Meditation (*Meditatio*)

After the reading, take some time to reflect in silence on one or more of the following questions:

- What word or words in this passage caught your attention?
- What in this passage comforted you?
- What in this passage challenged you?

If practicing lectio divina *as a family or in a group, after the reflection time, invite the participants to share their responses.*

Prayer (*Oratio*)

Read the scripture passage one more time. Bring to the Lord the praise, petition, or thanksgiving that the Word inspires in you.

Contemplation (*Contemplatio*)

Read the Scripture again, followed by this reflection:

 What conversion of mind, heart, and life is the Lord asking of me?

 "Hail, full of grace! The Lord is with you." At what times in my life have I felt the presence of God most strongly? When have I had an opportunity to accompany a brother or sister in Christ in a time of sorrow or joy?

She was greatly troubled at what was said. When have I struggled with Scripture or Church teaching? What resources do I have to keep me close to the truth?

May it be done to me according to your word. Am I docile to the promptings of the Holy Spirit? How can I conform my heart and mind to God's holy will?

After a period of silent reflection and/or discussion, all recite the Lord's Prayer and the following:

Closing Prayer

Sing to the LORD a new song,
    for he has done wondrous deeds;
His right hand has won victory for him,
    his holy arm.

The LORD has made his salvation known:
    in the sight of the nations he has revealed his justice.

He has remembered his kindness and his faithfulness
   toward the house of Israel.

All the ends of the earth have seen
   the salvation by our God.
Sing joyfully to the LORD, all you lands;
   break into song; sing praise.

From Psalm 98

Living the Word This Week

How can I make my life a gift for others in charity?

From now until Christmas, spend ten minutes a day reading
and praying with the Scriptures.

December 13, 2021

Lectio Divina for the Third Week of Advent

We begin our prayer:
In the name of the Father, and of the Son, and of the Holy Spirit. Amen.

Incline a merciful ear to our cry, we pray, O Lord,
and, casting light on the darkness of our hearts,
visit us with the grace of your Son.
Who lives and reigns with you in the unity of the Holy Spirit,
one God, for ever and ever.

Collect, Monday of the Third Week of Advent

Reading (*Lectio*)

Read the following Scripture two or three times.

John 1:6-8, 19-28

A man named John was sent from God. He came for testimony, to testify to the light, so that all might believe through him. He was not the light, but came to testify to the light.

And this is the testimony of John. When the Jews from Jerusalem sent priests and Levites to him to ask him, "Who are you?" He admitted and did not deny it, but admitted, "I am not the Christ." So they asked him, "What are you then? Are you Elijah?" And he said, "I am not." "Are you the Prophet?" He answered, "No." So they said to him, "Who are you, so we can give an answer to those who sent us? What do you have to say for yourself?" He said:

"I am *the voice of one crying out in the desert,*
  'make straight the way of the Lord,'

as Isaiah the prophet said." Some Pharisees were also sent. They asked him, "Why then do you baptize if you are not the Christ or Elijah or the Prophet?" John answered them, "I baptize with water; but there is one among you whom you do not recognize, the one who is coming after me, whose sandal strap I am not worthy to untie." This happened in Bethany across the Jordan, where John was baptizing.

Meditation (*Meditatio*)

After the reading, take some time to reflect in silence on one or more of the following questions:

- What word or words in this passage caught your attention?
- What in this passage comforted you?
- What in this passage challenged you?

If practicing lectio divina *as a family or in a group, after the reflection time, invite the participants to share their responses.*

Prayer (*Oratio*)

Read the scripture passage one more time. Bring to the Lord the praise, petition, or thanksgiving that the Word inspires in you.

Contemplation (*Contemplatio*)

Read the Scripture again, followed by this reflection:

 What conversion of mind, heart, and life is the Lord asking of me?

 He came for testimony, to testify to the light, so that all might believe through him. How do I share my faith with the people around me? What things keep me from sharing my faith?

 I am "*the voice of one crying out in the desert.*" When have my efforts to share my faith felt futile? How does God support me when I am discouraged?

There is one among you whom you do not recognize.
When have I encountered Jesus in disguise?
When have I failed to recognize Jesus in my life?

After a period of silent reflection and/or discussion, all recite the Lord's Prayer and the following:

Closing Prayer

My soul proclaims the greatness of the Lord;
    my spirit rejoices in God my Savior,
for he has looked upon his lowly servant.
    From this day all generations will call me blessed:

the Almighty has done great things for me,
    and holy is his Name.
He has mercy on those who fear him
    in every generation.

He has filled the hungry with good things,
    and the rich he has sent away empty.
He has come to the help of his servant Israel
    for he has remembered his promise of mercy,

From Luke 1

Living the Word This Week

How can I make my life a gift for others in charity?

Read *Disciples Called to Witness* (*http://www.usccb.org/beliefs-and-teachings/how-we-teach/new-evangelization/disciples-called-to-witness/upload/Disciples-Called-to-Witness-5-30-12.pdf*) and commit to sharing your faith with those you meet.

December 20, 2020

Lectio Divina for the Fourth Week of Advent

We begin our prayer:
In the name of the Father, and of the Son, and of the Holy
Spirit. Amen.

Hear in kindness, O Lord,
the prayers of your people,
that those who rejoice
at the coming of your Only Begotten Son in our flesh
may, when at last he comes in glory,
gain the reward of eternal life.
Through our Lord Jesus Christ, your Son,
who lives and reigns with you in the unity of the Holy Spirit,
one God, for ever and ever.

Collect, December 21

Reading (*Lectio*)

Read the following Scripture two or three times.

Luke 1:26-38

The angel Gabriel was sent from God to a town of
Galilee called Nazareth, to a virgin betrothed to
a man named Joseph, of the house of David, and the
virgin's name was Mary. And coming to her, he said,
"Hail, full of grace! The Lord is with you." But she was
greatly troubled at what was said and pondered what

sort of greeting this might be. Then the angel said to her, "Do not be afraid, Mary, for you have found favor with God.

"Behold, you will conceive in your womb and bear a son, and you shall name him Jesus. He will be great and will be called Son of the Most High, and the Lord God will give him the throne of David his father, and he will rule over the house of Jacob forever, and of his kingdom there will be no end." But Mary said to the angel, "How can this be, since I have no relations with a man?" And the angel said to her in reply, "The Holy Spirit will come upon you, and the power of the Most High will overshadow you. Therefore the child to be born will be called holy, the Son of God. And behold, Elizabeth, your relative, has also conceived a son in her old age, and this is the sixth month for her who was called barren; for nothing will be impossible for God." Mary said, "Behold, I am the handmaid of the Lord. May it be done to me according to your word." Then the angel departed from her.

Meditation (*Meditatio*)

After the reading, take some time to reflect in silence on one or more of the following questions:

- What word or words in this passage caught your attention?
- What in this passage comforted you?
- What in this passage challenged you?

If practicing lectio divina *as a family or in a group, after the reflection time, invite the participants to share their responses.*

Prayer (*Oratio*)

Read the scripture passage one more time. Bring to the Lord the praise, petition, or thanksgiving that the Word inspires in you.

Contemplation (*Contemplatio*)

Read the Scripture again, followed by this reflection:

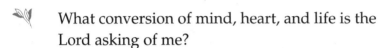 What conversion of mind, heart, and life is the Lord asking of me?

Do not be afraid. What fears keep me from living according to God's will? How can my faith help me to overcome those fears?

You have found favor with God. When have I felt God's favor in my life? How have I responded to the favor?

Therefore the child to be born will be called holy. How do I acknowledge God's holiness? How do I live my Christian call to holiness?

After a period of silent reflection and/or discussion, all recite the Lord's Prayer and the following:

Closing Prayer

The promises of the LORD I will sing forever;
    through all generations my mouth shall proclaim your
        faithfulness.
For you have said, "My kindness is established forever";
    in heaven you have confirmed your faithfulness.

"I have made a covenant with my chosen one,
    I have sworn to David my servant:
Forever will I confirm your posterity
    and establish your throne for all generations."

"He shall say of me, 'You are my father,
    my God, the Rock, my savior.'
Forever I will maintain my kindness toward him,
    and my covenant with him stands firm."

From Psalm 89

Living the Word This Week

How can I make my life a gift for others in charity?

If possible, spend some time this week in prayer before the Blessed Sacrament.

DECEMBER 25, 2020

Lectio Divina for the Solemnity of Christmas

We begin our prayer:
In the name of the Father, and of the Son, and of the Holy Spirit. Amen.

O God, who wonderfully created the dignity of human nature and still more wonderfully restored it,
grant, we pray,
that we may share in the divinity of Christ,
who humbled himself to share in our humanity.
Who lives and reigns with you in the unity of the Holy Spirit,
one God, for ever and ever.

Collect, Christmas, Mass during the Day

Reading (*Lectio*)

Read the following Scripture two or three times.

John 1:1-5, 9-14

In the beginning was the Word,
and the Word was with God,
and the Word was God.
He was in the beginning with God.
All things came to be through him,
and without him nothing came to be.
What came to be through him was life,
and this life was the light of the human race;

the light shines in the darkness,
and the darkness has not overcome it.

The true light, which enlightens everyone, was coming
into the world.
He was in the world,
and the world came to be through him,
but the world did not know him.
He came to what was his own,
but his own people did not accept him.
But to those who did accept him he gave power to
become children of God, to those who believe in his
name, who were born not by natural generation nor by
human choice nor by a man's decision but of God.
And the Word became flesh
and made his dwelling among us,
and we saw his glory,
the glory as of the Father's only Son,
full of grace and truth.

Meditation (*Meditatio*)

*After the reading, take some time to reflect in silence on one or more
of the following questions:*

- What word or words in this passage caught
  your attention?
- What in this passage comforted you?
- What in this passage challenged you?

If practicing lectio divina *as a family or in a group, after the
reflection time, invite the participants to share their responses.*

Prayer (*Oratio*)

Read the scripture passage one more time. Bring to the Lord the praise, petition, or thanksgiving that the Word inspires in you.

Contemplation (*Contemplatio*)

Read the Scripture again, followed by this reflection:

 What conversion of mind, heart, and life is the Lord asking of me?

 All things came to be through him. Do I receive all I have as a gift from God? How do I show my gratitude for God's gifts?

 The light shines in the darkness, / and the darkness has not overcome it. How can I share God's light in my life? What darkness in my life do I need God's grace to overcome?

The world did not know him. How did I come to know God? How can I help others know God?

After a period of silent reflection and/or discussion, all recite the Lord's Prayer and the following:

Closing Prayer

Sing to the LORD a new song,
    for he has done wondrous deeds;
his right hand has won victory for him,
    his holy arm.

The LORD has made his salvation known:
    in the sight of the nations he has revealed his justice.
He has remembered his kindness and his faithfulness
    toward the house of Israel.

All the ends of the earth have seen
    the salvation by our God.
Sing joyfully to the LORD, all you lands;
    break into song; sing praise.

Sing praise to the LORD with the harp,
    with the harp and melodious song.
With trumpets and the sound of the horn
    sing joyfully before the King, the LORD.

From Psalm 98

Living the Word This Week

How can I make my life a gift for others in charity?

Donate food, household goods, or money to those in need through Catholic Charities or the Saint Vincent de Paul Society.

December 27, 2020

Lectio Divina for the Feast of the Holy Family

We begin our prayer:
In the name of the Father, and of the Son, and of the Holy
Spirit. Amen.

O God, who were pleased to give us
the shining example of the Holy Family,
graciously grant that we may imitate them
in practicing the virtues of family life and in the bonds
  of charity,
and so, in the joy of your house,
delight one day in eternal rewards.
Through our Lord Jesus Christ, your Son,
who lives and reigns with you in the unity of the Holy Spirit,
one God, for ever and ever.

Collect, Feast of the Holy Family

Reading (*Lectio*)

Read the following Scripture two or three times.

Luke 2:22-40

When the days were completed for their
purification according to the law of Moses, They
took him up to Jerusalem to present him to the Lord,
just as it is written in the law of the Lord, *Every male
that opens the womb shall be consecrated to the Lord*, and

to offer the sacrifice of *a pair of turtledoves or two young pigeons*, in accordance with the dictate in the law of the Lord.

Now there was a man in Jerusalem whose name was Simeon. This man was righteous and devout, awaiting the consolation of Israel, and the Holy Spirit was upon him. It had been revealed to him by the Holy Spirit that he should not see death before he had seen the Christ of the Lord. He came in the Spirit into the temple; and when the parents brought in the child Jesus to perform the custom of the law in regard to him, he took him into his arms and blessed God, saying:

"Now, Master, you may let your servant go
    in peace, according to your word,
for my eyes have seen your salvation,
    which you prepared in sight of all the peoples,
a light for revelation to the Gentiles,
    and glory for your people Israel."

The child's father and mother were amazed at what was said about him; and Simeon blessed them and said to Mary his mother, "Behold, this child is destined for the fall and rise of many in Israel, and to be a sign that will be contradicted —and you yourself a sword will pierce— so that the thoughts of many hearts may be revealed." There was also a prophetess, Anna, the daughter of Phanuel, of the tribe of Asher. She was advanced in years, having lived seven years with her husband after her marriage, and then as a widow until she was eighty-four. She never left the temple, but worshiped night and day with fasting and prayer. And coming forward at that very time, she gave thanks to God and spoke about the child to all who were awaiting the redemption of Jerusalem.

When they had fulfilled all the prescriptions of the law of the Lord, they returned to Galilee, to their own town of Nazareth. The child grew and became strong, filled with wisdom; and the favor of God was upon him.

Meditation (*Meditatio*)

After the reading, take some time to reflect in silence on one or more of the following questions:

- What word or words in this passage caught your attention?
- What in this passage comforted you?
- What in this passage challenged you?

If practicing lectio divina *as a family or in a group, after the reflection time, invite the participants to share their responses.*

Prayer (*Oratio*)

Read the scripture passage one more time. Bring to the Lord the praise, petition, or thanksgiving that the Word inspires in you.

Contemplation (*Contemplatio*)

Read the Scripture again, followed by this reflection:

What conversion of mind, heart, and life is the Lord asking of me?

He came in the Spirit into the temple. How can I prepare my heart and mind to participate in the Eucharistic liturgy? How can I make participation in the Mass a more central part of my faith life?

A sign that will be contradicted. How does my faith challenge the values I see in the world around me? How can I grow stronger in my ability to follow Jesus instead of the world?

When they had fulfilled all the prescriptions of the law of the Lord. In what ways do I struggle to conform my life to God's plan? What graces do I need to follow God more closely?

After a period of silent reflection and/or discussion, all recite the Lord's Prayer and the following:

Closing Prayer

Give thanks to the LORD, invoke his name;
    make known among the nations his deeds.
Sing to him, sing his praise,
    proclaim all his wondrous deeds.

Glory in his holy name;
    rejoice, O hearts that seek the LORD!
Look to the LORD in his strength;
    constantly seek his face.

You descendants of Abraham, his servants,
    sons of Jacob, his chosen ones!
He, the LORD, is our God;
    throughout the earth his judgments prevail.

He remembers forever his covenant
    which he made binding for a thousand generations
which he entered into with Abraham
    and by his oath to Isaac.

From Psalm 105

Living the Word This Week

How can I make my life a gift for others in charity?

The next time you attend Mass, focus on paying close attention to the prayers and actions of the Mass, participating in body and spirit.

January 1, 2021

Lectio Divina for the Solemnity of Mary, Mother of God

We begin our prayer:
In the name of the Father, and of the Son, and of the Holy
Spirit. Amen.

O God, who are without beginning or end,
the source of all creation,
grant us so to live this new year,
whose beginning we dedicate to you,
that we may abound in good things
and be resplendent with works of holiness.
Through our Lord Jesus Christ, your Son,
who lives and reigns with you in the unity of the Holy Spirit,
one God, for ever and ever.

Collect, Mass at the Beginning of the Civil Year

Reading (*Lectio*)

Read the following Scripture two or three times.

Luke 2:16-21

The shepherds went in haste to Bethlehem and
found Mary and Joseph, and the infant lying in
the manger. When they saw this, they made known
the message that had been told them about this child.
All who heard it were amazed by what had been
told them by the shepherds. And Mary kept all these

things, reflecting on them in her heart. Then the
shepherds returned, glorifying and praising God for
all they had heard and seen, just as it had been told
to them.

When eight days were completed for his circumcision,
he was named Jesus, the name given him by the angel
before he was conceived in the womb.

Meditation (*Meditatio*)

*After the reading, take some time to reflect in silence on one or more
of the following questions:*

- What word or words in this passage caught
  your attention?
- What in this passage comforted you?
- What in this passage challenged you?

If practicing lectio divina *as a family or in a group, after the
reflection time, invite the participants to share their responses.*

Prayer (*Oratio*)

*Read the scripture passage one more time. Bring to the Lord the
praise, petition, or thanksgiving that the Word inspires in you.*

Contemplation (*Contemplatio*)

Read the Scripture again, followed by this reflection:

What conversion of mind, heart, and life is the
Lord asking of me?

The shepherds went in haste. Do I hasten to the Lord or rush past him? What keeps me from seeking the Lord and spending more time with him?

All who heard it were amazed by what had been told them by the shepherds. When have I felt amazement about God's action in my life? When have I been in awe of God's power and majesty?

Mary kept all these things, reflecting on them in her heart. What distractions keep me from reflecting on God's word? What places near me are most conducive to quiet prayer?

After a period of silent reflection and/or discussion, all recite the Lord's Prayer and the following:

Closing Prayer

May God have pity on us and bless us;
  may he let his face shine upon us.
So may your way be known upon earth;
  among all nations, your salvation.

May the nations be glad and exult
  because you rule the peoples in equity;
  the nations on the earth you guide.

May the peoples praise you, O God;
  may all the peoples praise you!
May God bless us,
  and may all the ends of the earth fear him

From Psalm 67

Living the Word This Week

How can I make my life a gift for others in charity?

Make a resolution to spend more time each week in prayer –
attending daily Mass, visiting the Blessed Sacrament, reading
Scripture, praying with family, or silent meditation.

January 3, 2021

Lectio Divina for the Solemnity of the Epiphany

We begin our prayer:
In the name of the Father, and of the Son, and of the Holy
Spirit. Amen.

Almighty ever-living God,
who through your Only Begotten Son
have made us a new creation for yourself,
grant, we pray,
that by your grace we may be found in the likeness of him,
in whom our nature is united to you.
Who lives and reigns with you in the unity of the Holy Spirit,
one God, for ever and ever.

Collect, Saturday after Epiphany

Reading (*Lectio*)

Read the following Scripture two or three times.

Matthew 2:1-12

When Jesus was born in Bethlehem of Judea, in the
days of King Herod, behold, magi from the east
arrived in Jerusalem, saying, "Where is the newborn
king of the Jews? We saw his star at its rising and have
come to do him homage." When King Herod heard
this, he was greatly troubled, and all Jerusalem with
him. Assembling all the chief priests and the scribes of

the people, he inquired of them where the Christ was to be born. They said to him, "In Bethlehem of Judea, for thus it has been written through the prophet:

And you, Bethlehem, land of Judah,
*   are by no means least among the rulers of Judah;*
since from you shall come a ruler,
*   who is to shepherd my people Israel."*

Then Herod called the magi secretly and ascertained from them the time of the star's appearance. He sent them to Bethlehem and said, "Go and search diligently for the child.

When you have found him, bring me word, that I too may go and do him homage." After their audience with the king they set out. And behold, the star that they had seen at its rising preceded them, until it came and stopped over the place where the child was. They were overjoyed at seeing the star, and on entering the house they saw the child with Mary his mother. They prostrated themselves and did him homage. Then they opened their treasures and offered him gifts of gold, frankincense, and myrrh. And having been warned in a dream not to return to Herod, they departed for their country by another way.

Meditation (*Meditatio*)

After the reading, take some time to reflect in silence on one or more of the following questions:

- What word or words in this passage caught your attention?

- What in this passage comforted you?
- What in this passage challenged you?

If practicing lectio divina *as a family or in a group, after the reflection time, invite the participants to share their responses.*

Prayer (*Oratio*)

Read the scripture passage one more time. Bring to the Lord the praise, petition, or thanksgiving that the Word inspires in you.

Contemplation (*Contemplatio*)

Read the Scripture again, followed by this reflection:

 What conversion of mind, heart, and life is the Lord asking of me?

 When you have found him, bring me word. Who was the first person who shared knowledge of Christ with me? With whom have I shared Christ?

Then they opened their treasures and offered him gifts of gold, frankincense, and myrrh. What gifts do I have to offer the Lord? How can I place these gifts at the service of God and God's people?

And having been warned in a dream not to return to Herod, they departed for their country by another way. What people, places, or things turn me away from the Lord? How can I find another way so that I can avoid these things?

After a period of silent reflection and/or discussion, all recite the Lord's Prayer and the following:

Closing Prayer

O God, with your judgment endow the king,
    and with your justice, the king's son;
He shall govern your people with justice
    and your afflicted ones with judgment.

Justice shall flower in his days,
   and profound peace, till the moon be no more.
May he rule from sea to sea, and from the River to the ends
      of the earth.

The kings of Tarshish and the Isles shall offer gifts;
   the kings of Arabia and Seba shall bring tribute.
All kings shall pay him homage,
   all nations shall serve him.

For he shall rescue the poor when he cries out,
   and the afflicted when he has no one to help him.
He shall have pity for the lowly and the poor;
   the lives of the poor he shall save.

From Psalm 72

Living the Word This Week

How can I make my life a gift for others in charity?

Look at the volunteer opportunities available in your parish
and community and find a way to share your gifts.

January 10, 2021

Lectio Divina for the Feast of the Baptism of the Lord

We begin our prayer:
In the name of the Father, and of the Son, and of the Holy
Spirit. Amen.

Almighty ever-living God,
who, when Christ had been baptized in the River Jordan
and as the Holy Spirit descended upon him,
solemnly declared him your beloved Son,
grant that your children by adoption,
reborn of water and the Holy Spirit,
may always be well pleasing to you.
Through our Lord Jesus Christ, your Son,
who lives and reigns with you in the unity of the Holy Spirit,
one God, for ever and ever.

Collect, Baptism of the Lord

Reading (*Lectio*)

Read the following Scripture two or three times.

Mark 1:7-11

This is what John the Baptist proclaimed: "One
mightier than I is coming after me. I am not worthy
to stoop and loosen the thongs of his sandals. I have
baptized you with water; he will baptize you with the
Holy Spirit."

It happened in those days that Jesus came from Nazareth of Galilee and was baptized in the Jordan by John. On coming up out of the water he saw the heavens being torn open and the Spirit, like a dove, descending upon him. And a voice came from the heavens, "You are my beloved Son; with you I am well pleased."

Meditation (*Meditatio*)

After the reading, take some time to reflect in silence on one or more of the following questions:

- What word or words in this passage caught your attention?
- What in this passage comforted you?
- What in this passage challenged you?

If practicing lectio divina *as a family or in a group, after the reflection time, invite the participants to share their responses.*

Prayer (*Oratio*)

Read the scripture passage one more time. Bring to the Lord the praise, petition, or thanksgiving that the Word inspires in you.

Contemplation (*Contemplatio*)

Read the Scripture again, followed by this reflection:

 What conversion of mind, heart, and life is the Lord asking of me?

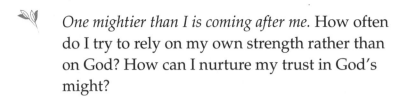 *One mightier than I is coming after me.* How often do I try to rely on my own strength rather than on God? How can I nurture my trust in God's might?

I am not worthy to stoop and loosen the thongs of his sandals. How am I called to serve God? How can I grow in humility?

You are my beloved Son; with you I am well pleased. When have I felt most beloved by God? How can I make my life a more pleasing sacrifice to God?

After a period of silent reflection and/or discussion, all recite the Lord's Prayer and the following:

Closing Prayer

God indeed is my savior;
    I am confident and unafraid.
My strength and my courage is the LORD,
    and he has been my savior.
With joy you will draw water
    at the fountain of salvation.

Give thanks to the LORD, acclaim his name;
    among the nations make known his deeds,
    proclaim how exalted is his name.

Sing praise to the LORD for his glorious achievement;
    let this be known throughout all the earth.
Shout with exultation, O city of Zion,
    for great in your midst
    is the Holy One of Israel!

From Isaiah 12

Living the Word This Week

How can I make my life a gift for others in charity?

Recall your Baptism by praying the Apostles' Creed: *http://ccc. usccb.org/flipbooks/uscca/#560/z.*

January 17, 2021

Lectio Divina for the Second Week in Ordinary Time

We begin our prayer:
In the name of the Father, and of the Son, and of the Holy
Spirit. Amen.

Almighty ever-living God,
who govern all things,
both in heaven and on earth,
mercifully hear the pleading of your people
and bestow your peace on our times.
Through our Lord Jesus Christ, your Son,
who lives and reigns with you in the unity of the Holy Spirit,
one God, for ever and ever.

Collect, Second Sunday in Ordinary Time

Reading (*Lectio*)

Read the following Scripture two or three times.

John 1:35-42

John was standing with two of his disciples, and
as he watched Jesus walk by, he said, "Behold,
the Lamb of God." The two disciples heard what
he said and followed Jesus. Jesus turned and saw
them following him and said to them, "What are
you looking for?" They said to him, "Rabbi"—which
translated means Teacher—, "where are you staying?"

He said to them, "Come, and you will see." So they went and saw where Jesus was staying, and they stayed with him that day. It was about four in the afternoon. Andrew, the brother of Simon Peter, was one of the two who heard John and followed Jesus. He first found his own brother Simon and told him, "We have found the Messiah"—which is translated Christ—. Then he brought him to Jesus. Jesus looked at him and said, "You are Simon the son of John; you will be called Cephas"—which is translated Peter.

Meditation (*Meditatio*)

After the reading, take some time to reflect in silence on one or more of the following questions:

- What word or words in this passage caught your attention?
- What in this passage comforted you?
- What in this passage challenged you?

If practicing lectio divina *as a family or in a group, after the reflection time, invite the participants to share their responses.*

Prayer (*Oratio*)

Read the scripture passage one more time. Bring to the Lord the praise, petition, or thanksgiving that the Word inspires in you.

Contemplation (*Contemplatio*)

Read the Scripture again, followed by this reflection:

What conversion of mind, heart, and life is the Lord asking of me?

The two disciples heard what he said and followed Jesus. How have I heard the voice of the Lord? How can I follow Jesus more closely?

What are you looking for? What am I looking for? Am I looking for things that truly matter?

Come, and you will see. How can I respond more wholeheartedly to the Lord's invitation? How can I extend that invitation to others?

After a period of silent reflection and/or discussion, all recite the Lord's Prayer and the following:

Closing Prayer

I have waited, waited for the LORD,
   and he stooped toward me and heard my cry.
And he put a new song into my mouth,
   a hymn to our God.

Sacrifice or offering you wished not,
   but ears open to obedience you gave me.
Holocausts or sin-offerings you sought not;
   then said I, "Behold I come."

"In the written scroll it is prescribed for me,
to do your will, O my God, is my delight,
   and your law is within my heart!"

I announced your justice in the vast assembly;
   I did not restrain my lips, as you, O LORD, know.

From Psalm 40

Living the Word This Week

How can I make my life a gift for others in charity?

Contact your parish or diocesan pro-life committee to find out how you can support a culture of life from conception until natural death.

January 24, 2021

Lectio Divina for the Third Week in Ordinary Time

We begin our prayer:
In the name of the Father, and of the Son, and of the Holy Spirit. Amen.

Almighty ever-living God,
direct our actions according to your good pleasure,
that in the name of your beloved Son
we may abound in good works.
Through our Lord Jesus Christ, your Son,
who lives and reigns with you in the unity of the Holy Spirit,
one God, for ever and ever.

Collect, Third Sunday in Ordinary Time

Reading (*Lectio*)

Read the following Scripture two or three times.

Mark 1:14-20

After John had been arrested, Jesus came to Galilee proclaiming the gospel of God: "This is the time of fulfillment. The kingdom of God is at hand. Repent, and believe in the gospel."

As he passed by the Sea of Galilee, he saw Simon and his brother Andrew casting their nets into the sea; they were fishermen. Jesus said to them, "Come after me, and I will make you fishers of men." Then they abandoned their nets and followed him. He walked along a little farther and saw James, the son of Zebedee, and his brother John. They too were in a boat mending their nets. Then he called them. So they left their father Zebedee in the boat along with the hired men and followed him.

Meditation (*Meditatio*)

After the reading, take some time to reflect in silence on one or more of the following questions:

- What word or words in this passage caught your attention?
- What in this passage comforted you?
- What in this passage challenged you?

If practicing lectio divina *as a family or in a group, after the reflection time, invite the participants to share their responses.*

Prayer (*Oratio*)

Read the scripture passage one more time. Bring to the Lord the praise, petition, or thanksgiving that the Word inspires in you.

Contemplation (*Contemplatio*)

Read the Scripture again, followed by this reflection:

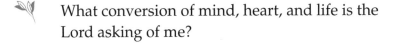 What conversion of mind, heart, and life is the Lord asking of me?

Jesus came to Galilee proclaiming the gospel of God. How do I proclaim the gospel of God by my words and actions? How can my proclamation be more authentic?

Repent, and believe in the gospel. How can I nurture a spirit of true repentance? How can I increase in trust of God's mercy?

Then they abandoned their nets and followed him. What am I willing to give up for the Lord? What prevents me from following the Lord wholeheartedly?

After a period of silent reflection and/or discussion, all recite the Lord's Prayer and the following:

Closing Prayer

Your ways, O LORD, make known to me;
    teach me your paths,
Guide me in your truth and teach me,
    for you are God my savior.

Remember that your compassion, O LORD,
    and your love are from of old.
In your kindness remember me,
    because of your goodness, O LORD.

Good and upright is the LORD;
    thus he shows sinners the way.
He guides the humble to justice
    and teaches the humble his way.

From Psalm 25

Living the Word This Week

How can I make my life a gift for others in charity?

Pray for those men and women in your diocese who are discerning vocations to the priesthood, diaconate, and consecrated life.

JANUARY 31, 2021

Lectio Divina for the Fourth Week in Ordinary Time

We begin our prayer:
In the name of the Father, and of the Son, and of the Holy
Spirit. Amen.

Grant us, Lord our God,
that we may honor you with all our mind,
and love everyone in truth of heart.
Through our Lord Jesus Christ, your Son,
who lives and reigns with you in the unity of the Holy Spirit,
one God, for ever and ever.

Collect, Fourth Sunday in Ordinary Time

Reading (*Lectio*)

Read the following Scripture two or three times.

Mark 1:21-28

Then they came to Capernaum, and on the sabbath
Jesus entered the synagogue and taught. The
people were astonished at his teaching, for he taught
them as one having authority and not as the scribes.
In their synagogue was a man with an unclean spirit;
he cried out, "What have you to do with us, Jesus of
Nazareth? Have you come to destroy us? I know who
you are—the Holy One of God!" Jesus rebuked him
and said, "Quiet! Come out of him!" The unclean

spirit convulsed him and with a loud cry came out of him. All were amazed and asked one another, "What is this? A new teaching with authority. He commands even the unclean spirits and they obey him." His fame spread everywhere throughout the whole region of Galilee.

Meditation (*Meditatio*)

After the reading, take some time to reflect in silence on one or more of the following questions:

- What word or words in this passage caught your attention?
- What in this passage comforted you?
- What in this passage challenged you?

If practicing lectio divina *as a family or in a group, after the reflection time, invite the participants to share their responses.*

Prayer (*Oratio*)

Read the scripture passage one more time. Bring to the Lord the praise, petition, or thanksgiving that the Word inspires in you.

Contemplation (*Contemplatio*)

Read the Scripture again, followed by this reflection:

 What conversion of mind, heart, and life is the Lord asking of me?

On the sabbath Jesus entered the synagogue and taught. How do I keep the Lord's day holy and free of unnecessary work? How can I keep Mass and the sacraments as a priority in my life?

I know who you are—the Holy One of God! How do I grow in my knowledge of the Lord? How can I accompany others on their journey to know Jesus?

What is this? A new teaching with authority. What resources are available to help me learn more about what the Church teaches? What is my proper response to authority?

After a period of silent reflection and/or discussion, all recite the Lord's Prayer and the following:

Closing Prayer

Come, let us sing joyfully to the Lord;
   let us acclaim the rock of our salvation.
Let us come into his presence with thanksgiving;
   let us joyfully sing psalms to him.

Come, let us bow down in worship;
   let us kneel before the Lord who made us.
For he is our God,
   and we are the people he shepherds, the flock he guides.

Oh, that today you would hear his voice:
   "Harden not your hearts as at Meribah,
   as in the day of Massah in the desert,
Where your fathers tempted me;
   they tested me though they had seen my works."

From Psalm 95

Living the Word This Week

How can I make my life a gift for others in charity?

Commit to learning more about your faith by attending a class in your parish or diocese or reading good Catholic books.

February 7, 2021

Lectio Divina for the Fifth Week in Ordinary Time

We begin our prayer:
In the name of the Father, and of the Son, and of the Holy
Spirit. Amen.

Keep your family safe, O Lord, with unfailing care,
that, relying solely on the hope of heavenly grace,
they may be defended always by your protection.
Through our Lord Jesus Christ, your Son,
who lives and reigns with you in the unity of the Holy Spirit,
one God, for ever and ever.

Collect, Fifth Week in Ordinary Time

Reading (*Lectio*)

Read the following Scripture two or three times.

Mark 1:29-39

On leaving the synagogue Jesus entered the house
of Simon and Andrew with James and John.
Simon's mother-in-law lay sick with a fever. They
immediately told him about her. He approached,
grasped her hand, and helped her up. Then the fever
left her and she waited on them. When it was evening,
after sunset, they brought to him all who were ill or
possessed by demons.

The whole town was gathered at the door. He cured many who were sick with various diseases, and he drove out many demons, not permitting them to speak because they knew him.

Rising very early before dawn, he left and went off to a deserted place, where he prayed. Simon and those who were with him pursued him and on finding him said, "Everyone is looking for you." He told them, "Let us go on to the nearby villages that I may preach there also. For this purpose have I come." So he went into their synagogues, preaching and driving out demons throughout the whole of Galilee.

Meditation (*Meditatio*)

After the reading, take some time to reflect in silence on one or more of the following questions:

- What word or words in this passage caught your attention?
- What in this passage comforted you?
- What in this passage challenged you?

If practicing lectio divina *as a family or in a group, after the reflection time, invite the participants to share their responses.*

Prayer (*Oratio*)

Read the scripture passage one more time. Bring to the Lord the praise, petition, or thanksgiving that the Word inspires in you.

Contemplation (*Contemplatio*)

Read the Scripture again, followed by this reflection:

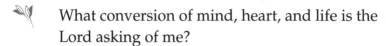 What conversion of mind, heart, and life is the Lord asking of me?

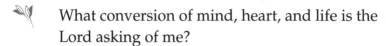 *He approached, grasped her hand, and helped her up.* How can I help to lift others up? Who in my life is in need of support?

 He left and went off to a deserted place, where he prayed. What things distract me from prayer? How can I quiet or remove those distractions?

For this purpose have I come. To what purpose is God calling me? How can I discern my life's purpose?

After a period of silent reflection and/or discussion, all recite the Lord's Prayer and the following:

Closing Prayer

Praise the LORD, for he is good;
    sing praise to our God, for he is gracious;
    it is fitting to praise him.
The LORD rebuilds Jerusalem;
    the dispersed of Israel he gathers.

He heals the brokenhearted
    and binds up their wounds.
He tells the number of the stars;
    he calls each by name.

Great is our Lord and mighty in power;
    to his wisdom there is no limit.
The LORD sustains the lowly;
    the wicked he casts to the ground.

From Psalm 147

Living the Word This Week

How can I make my life a gift for others in charity?

Pray for those who are sick and those who provide their care. Consider participating in your parish's ministry to the homebound by offering companionship, food, or regular contact.

FEBRUARY 14, 2021

Lectio Divina for the Sixth Week in Ordinary Time

We begin our prayer:
In the name of the Father, and of the Son, and of the Holy Spirit. Amen.

O God, who teach us that you abide
in hearts that are just and true,
grant that we may be so fashioned by your grace
as to become a dwelling pleasing to you.
Through our Lord Jesus Christ, your Son,
who lives and reigns with you in the unity of the Holy Spirit,
one God, for ever and ever.

Collect, Sixth Sunday in Ordinary Time

Reading (*Lectio*)

Read the following Scripture two or three times.

Mark 1:40-45

A leper came to Jesus and kneeling down begged him and said, "If you wish, you can make me clean." Moved with pity, he stretched out his hand, touched him, and said to him, "I do will it. Be made clean." The leprosy left him immediately, and he was made clean. Then, warning him sternly, he dismissed him at once.

He said to him, "See that you tell no one anything, but go, show yourself to the priest and offer for your cleansing what Moses prescribed; that will be proof for them."

The man went away and began to publicize the whole matter. He spread the report abroad so that it was impossible for Jesus to enter a town openly. He remained outside in deserted places, and people kept coming to him from everywhere.

Meditation (*Meditatio*)

After the reading, take some time to reflect in silence on one or more of the following questions:

- What word or words in this passage caught your attention?
- What in this passage comforted you?
- What in this passage challenged you?

If practicing lectio divina *as a family or in a group, after the reflection time, invite the participants to share their responses.*

Prayer (*Oratio*)

Read the scripture passage one more time. Bring to the Lord the praise, petition, or thanksgiving that the Word inspires in you.

Contemplation (*Contemplatio*)

Read the Scripture again, followed by this reflection:

What conversion of mind, heart, and life is the Lord asking of me?

A leper came to Jesus and kneeling down begged him. For what do I need to beg Jesus? How can I approach Jesus in reverence and humility?

Moved with pity, he stretched out his hand. What encourages me to reach out to those in need? How can I grow in compassion?

That will be proof for them. How do I deal with those who question my faith? How can I support and defend what I believe?

After a period of silent reflection and/or discussion, all recite the Lord's Prayer and the following:

Closing Prayer

Blessed is he whose fault is taken away,
　　whose sin is covered.
Blessed the man to whom the LORD imputes not guilt,
　　in whose spirit there is no guile.

Then I acknowledged my sin to you,
　　my guilt I covered not.
I said, "I confess my faults to the LORD,"
　　and you took away the guilt of my sin.

Be glad in the LORD and rejoice, you just;
　　exult, all you upright of heart.

From Psalm 32

Living the Word This Week

How can I make my life a gift for others in charity?

Bring your needs and the needs of the world to Jesus in prayer before the Blessed Sacrament.

February 17, 2021

Lectio Divina for Ash Wednesday

We begin our prayer:
In the name of the Father, and of the Son, and of the Holy Spirit. Amen.

Show gracious favor, O Lord, we pray,
to the works of penance we have begun,
that we may have strength to accomplish with sincerity
the bodily observances we undertake.
Through our Lord Jesus Christ, your Son,
who lives and reigns with you in the unity of the Holy Spirit,
one God, for ever and ever.

Collect, Friday after Ash Wednesday

Reading (*Lectio*)

Read the following Scripture two or three times.

Matthew 6:1-6, 16-18

Jesus said to his disciples: "Take care not to perform righteous deeds in order that people may see them; otherwise, you will have no recompense from your heavenly Father. When you give alms, do not blow a trumpet before you, as the hypocrites do in the synagogues and in the streets to win the praise of others. Amen, I say to you, they have received their reward. But when you give alms, do not let your left hand know what your right is doing, so that your almsgiving may be secret. And your Father who sees in secret will repay you.

"When you pray, do not be like the hypocrites, who love to stand and pray in the synagogues and on street corners so that others may see them. Amen, I say to you, they have received their reward. But when you pray, go to your inner room, close the door, and pray to your Father in secret. And your Father who sees in secret will repay you.

"When you fast, do not look gloomy like the hypocrites. They neglect their appearance, so that they may appear to others to be fasting. Amen, I say to you, they have received their reward.

But when you fast, anoint your head and wash your face, so that you may not appear to be fasting, except to your Father who is hidden. And your Father who sees what is hidden will repay you."

Meditation (*Meditatio*)

After the reading, take some time to reflect in silence on one or more of the following questions:

- What word or words in this passage caught your attention?
- What in this passage comforted you?
- What in this passage challenged you?

If practicing lectio divina *as a family or in a group, after the reflection time, invite the participants to share their responses.*

Prayer (*Oratio*)

Read the scripture passage one more time. Bring to the Lord the praise, petition, or thanksgiving that the Word inspires in you.

Contemplation (*Contemplatio*)

Read the Scripture again, followed by this reflection:

 What conversion of mind, heart, and life is the Lord asking of me?

 Take care not to perform righteous deeds in order that people may see them. What righteous deeds do I need to perform? What motivates me to do what is good?

 When you pray, go to your inner room, close the door, and pray to your Father in secret. What forms of

prayer are most spiritually fulfilling to me? For
what do I need to pray this Lent?

Do not look gloomy like the hypocrites. Does my
relationship with God and his Church bring me
joy? How can I share the joy of the Gospel?

*After a period of silent reflection and/or discussion, all recite the
Lord's Prayer and the following:*

Closing Prayer

Have mercy on me, O God, in your goodness;
  in the greatness of your compassion wipe out my offense.
Thoroughly wash me from my guilt
  and of my sin cleanse me.

For I acknowledge my offense,
  and my sin is before me always:
"Against you only have I sinned,
  and done what is evil in your sight."

A clean heart create for me, O God,
    and a steadfast spirit renew within me.
Cast me not out from your presence,
    and your Holy Spirit take not from me.

Give me back the joy of your salvation,
    and a willing spirit sustain in me.
O Lord, open my lips,
    and my mouth shall proclaim your praise.

From Psalm 51

Living the Word This Week

How can I make my life a gift for others in charity?

Commit to lenten practices of prayer, fasting, and almsgiving.

February 21, 2021

Lectio Divina for the First Week of Lent

We begin our prayer:
In the name of the Father, and of the Son, and of the Holy
Spirit. Amen.

Bestow on us, we pray, O Lord,
a spirit of always pondering on what is right
and of hastening to carry it out,
and, since without you we cannot exist,
may we be enabled to live according to your will.
Through our Lord Jesus Christ, your Son,
who lives and reigns with you in the unity of the Holy Spirit,
one God, for ever and ever.

Collect, Thursday of the First Week of Lent

Reading (*Lectio*)

Read the following Scripture two or three times.

Mark 1:12-15

The Spirit drove Jesus out into the desert, and he
remained in the desert for forty days, tempted
by Satan. He was among wild beasts, and the angels
ministered to him.

After John had been arrested, Jesus came to Galilee
proclaiming the gospel of God: "This is the time of

fulfillment. The kingdom of God is at hand. Repent, and believe in the gospel."

Meditation (*Meditatio*)

After the reading, take some time to reflect in silence on one or more of the following questions:

- What word or words in this passage caught your attention?
- What in this passage comforted you?
- What in this passage challenged you?

If practicing lectio divina *as a family or in a group, after the reflection time, invite the participants to share their responses.*

Prayer (*Oratio*)

Read the scripture passage one more time. Bring to the Lord the praise, petition, or thanksgiving that the Word inspires in you.

Contemplation (*Contemplatio*)

Read the Scripture again, followed by this reflection:

 What conversion of mind, heart, and life is the Lord asking of me?

He remained in the desert for forty days, tempted by Satan. When have I wandered far away from God? What tempts me to sinful behaviors?

The angels ministered to him. When have I felt the consolation of God's love? How can I share that love with those I meet?

Repent, and believe in the gospel. What parts of my life are in need of conversion? How can I grow in my ability to follow God's will for my life?

After a period of silent reflection and/or discussion, all recite the Lord's Prayer and the following:

Closing Prayer

Your ways, O Lord, make known to me;
    teach me your paths,
Guide me in your truth and teach me,
    for you are God my savior.

Remember that your compassion, O Lord,
    and your love are from of old.
In your kindness remember me,
    because of your goodness, O Lord.

Good and upright is the Lord,
    thus he shows sinners the way.
He guides the humble to justice,
    and he teaches the humble his way.

From Psalm 25

Living the Word This Week

How can I make my life a gift for others in charity?

Make plans to receive the Sacrament of Penance during Lent.

February 28, 2021

Lectio Divina for the Second Week of Lent

We begin our prayer:
In the name of the Father, and of the Son, and of the Holy Spirit. Amen.

O God, who have commanded us
to listen to your beloved Son,
be pleased, we pray,
to nourish us inwardly by your word,
that, with spiritual sight made pure,
we may rejoice to behold your glory.
Through our Lord Jesus Christ, your Son,
who lives and reigns with you in the unity of the Holy Spirit,
one God, for ever and ever.

Collect, Second Sunday of Lent

Reading (*Lectio*)

Read the following Scripture two or three times.

Mark 9:2-10

Jesus took Peter, James, and John and led them up a high mountain apart by themselves. And he was transfigured before them, and his clothes became dazzling white, such as no fuller on earth could bleach them. Then Elijah appeared to them along with Moses, and they were conversing with Jesus. Then Peter said to Jesus in reply, "Rabbi, it is good that we are here! Let us make three tents: one for you, one for Moses, and one for Elijah." He hardly knew what to say, they were so terrified. Then a cloud came, casting a shadow over them; from the cloud came a voice, "This is my beloved Son. Listen to him." Suddenly, looking around, they no longer saw anyone but Jesus alone with them.

As they were coming down from the mountain, he charged them not to relate what they had seen to anyone, except when the Son of Man had risen from the dead. So they kept the matter to themselves, questioning what rising from the dead meant.

Meditation (*Meditatio*)

After the reading, take some time to reflect in silence on one or more of the following questions:

- What word or words in this passage caught your attention?
- What in this passage comforted you?
- What in this passage challenged you?

If practicing lectio divina *as a family or in a group, after the reflection time, invite the participants to share their responses.*

Prayer (*Oratio*)

Read the scripture passage one more time. Bring to the Lord the praise, petition, or thanksgiving that the Word inspires in you.

Contemplation (*Contemplatio*)

Read the Scripture again, followed by this reflection:

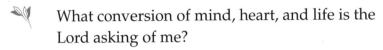 What conversion of mind, heart, and life is the Lord asking of me?

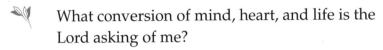 *Jesus . . . led them up a high mountain apart by themselves.* Where do I find quiet and peace to pray? What distracts me from focusing on God?

 Rabbi, it is good that we are here! Where do I feel the presence of God most clearly? Where do I need to share Christ's presence?

So they kept the matter to themselves. When have I failed to speak out about my faith? Who needs me to speak a word of hope?

After a period of silent reflection and/or discussion, all recite the Lord's Prayer and the following:

Closing Prayer

I believed, even when I said,
   "I am greatly afflicted."
Precious in the eyes of the LORD
   is the death of his faithful ones.

O LORD, I am your servant;
   I am your servant, the son of your handmaid;
      you have loosed my bonds.
To you will I offer sacrifice of thanksgiving,
   and I will call upon the name of the LORD.

My vows to the LORD I will pay
   in the presence of all his people,
In the courts of the house of the LORD,
   in your midst, O Jerusalem.

From Psalm 116

Living the Word This Week

How can I make my life a gift for others in charity?

Reach out to someone who is in need of a word of hope or encouragement.

March 7, 2021

Lectio Divina for the Third Week of Lent

We begin our prayer:
In the name of the Father, and of the Son, and of the Holy Spirit. Amen.

Pour your grace into our hearts, we pray, O Lord,
that we may be constantly drawn away from unruly desires
and obey by your own gift the heavenly teaching you give us.
Through our Lord Jesus Christ, your Son,
who lives and reigns with you in the unity of the Holy Spirit,
one God, for ever and ever.

Collect, Friday of the Third Week of Lent

Reading (*Lectio*)

Read the following Scripture two or three times.

John 2:13-25

Since the Passover of the Jews was near, Jesus went up to Jerusalem. He found in the temple area those who sold oxen, sheep, and doves, as well as the money changers seated there. He made a whip out of cords and drove them all out of the temple area, with the sheep and oxen, and spilled the coins of the money changers and overturned their tables, and to those who sold doves he said, "Take these out of here, and stop making my Father's house a marketplace." His disciples recalled the words of Scripture, *Zeal for your house will consume me.* At this the Jews answered and said to him, "What sign can you show us for doing this?" Jesus answered and said to them, "Destroy this temple and in three days I will raise it up." The Jews said, "This temple has been under construction for forty-six years, and you will raise it up in three days?" But he was speaking about the temple of his body. Therefore, when he was raised from the dead, his disciples remembered that he had said this, and they came to believe the Scripture and the word Jesus had spoken.

While he was in Jerusalem for the feast of Passover, many began to believe in his name when they saw the signs he was doing. But Jesus would not trust himself to them because he knew them all, and did not need anyone to testify about human nature. He himself understood it well.

Meditation (*Meditatio*)

After the reading, take some time to reflect in silence on one or more of the following questions:

- What word or words in this passage caught your attention?
- What in this passage comforted you?
- What in this passage challenged you?

If practicing lectio divina *as a family or in a group, after the reflection time, invite the participants to share their responses.*

Prayer (*Oratio*)

Read the scripture passage one more time. Bring to the Lord the praise, petition, or thanksgiving that the Word inspires in you.

Contemplation (*Contemplatio*)

Read the Scripture again, followed by this reflection:

 What conversion of mind, heart, and life is the Lord asking of me?

 Stop making my Father's house a marketplace. How do temporal concerns distract me from the things of God? How does love of money and possessions keep me from loving God wholeheartedly?

 Zeal for your house will consume me. How important is my relationship with God in my daily life? How do I prioritize prayer, worship and acts of charity?

Many began to believe in his name when they saw the signs he was doing. What strengthens my faith? How can my words and actions share the Gospel with the people I meet?

After a period of silent reflection and/or discussion, all recite the Lord's Prayer and the following:

Closing Prayer

The law of the LORD is perfect,
   refreshing the soul;
The decree of the LORD is trustworthy,
   giving wisdom to the simple.

The precepts of the LORD are right,
   rejoicing the heart;
the command of the LORD is clear,
   enlightening the eye.

The fear of the LORD is pure,
 enduring forever;
the ordinances of the LORD are true,
 all of them just.

They are more precious than gold,
 than a heap of purest gold;
sweeter also than syrup
 or honey from the comb.

From Psalm 19

Living the Word This Week

How can I make my life a gift for others in charity?

Invite someone to join you for Mass or a lenten devotion or program at your church.

MARCH 14, 2021

Lectio Divina for the Fourth Week of Lent

We begin our prayer:
In the name of the Father, and of the Son, and of the Holy
Spirit. Amen.

May the working of your mercy, O Lord, we pray,
direct our hearts aright,
for without your grace
we cannot find favor in your sight.
Through our Lord Jesus Christ, your Son,
who lives and reigns with you in the unity of the Holy Spirit,
one God, for ever and ever.

Collect, Saturday of the Fourth Week of Lent

Reading (*Lectio*)

Read the following Scripture two or three times.

John 3:14-21

Jesus said to Nicodemus: "Just as Moses lifted up
the serpent in the desert, so must the Son of Man be
lifted up, so that everyone who believes in him may
have eternal life."

For God so loved the world that he gave his only Son,
so that everyone who believes in him might not perish
but might have eternal life. For God did not send his

Son into the world to condemn the world, but that the world might be saved through him. Whoever believes in him will not be condemned, but whoever does not believe has already been condemned, because he has not believed in the name of the only Son of God. And this is the verdict, that the light came into the world, but people preferred darkness to light, because their works were evil. For everyone who does wicked things hates the light and does not come toward the light, so that his works might not be exposed. But whoever lives the truth comes to the light, so that his works may be clearly seen as done in God.

Meditation (*Meditatio*)

After the reading, take some time to reflect in silence on one or more of the following questions:

- What word or words in this passage caught your attention?
- What in this passage comforted you?
- What in this passage challenged you?

If practicing lectio divina *as a family or in a group, after the reflection time, invite the participants to share their responses.*

Prayer (*Oratio*)

Read the scripture passage one more time. Bring to the Lord the praise, petition, or thanksgiving that the Word inspires in you.

Contemplation (*Contemplatio*)

Read the Scripture again, followed by this reflection:

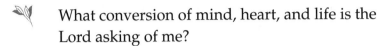 What conversion of mind, heart, and life is the Lord asking of me?

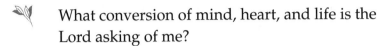 *So must the Son of Man be lifted up, so that everyone who believes in him may have eternal life.* What needs should I lift up to God? How can I carry my cross as a disciple?

 For God so loved the world that he gave his only Son. When have I felt God's love most clearly? How can I share God's love with the people I meet?

But whoever lives the truth comes to the light, so that his works may be clearly seen as done in God. How am I forming my conscience to know God's truth? What parts of my life need to be brought into God's light?

After a period of silent reflection and/or discussion, all recite the Lord's Prayer and the following:

Closing Prayer

By the streams of Babylon
    we sat and wept
        when we remembered Zion.
On the aspens of that land
    we hung up our harps.

For there our captors asked of us
    the lyrics of our songs,
And our despoilers urged us to be joyous:
    "Sing for us the songs of Zion!"

How could we sing a song of the LORD
    in a foreign land?
If I forget you, Jerusalem,
    may my right hand be forgotten!

May my tongue cleave to my palate
    if I remember you not,
If I place not Jerusalem
    ahead of my joy.

From Psalm 137

Living the Word This Week

How can I make my life a gift for others in charity?

Offer the daily crosses in your life for the needs of the world.

MARCH 21, 2021

Lectio Divina for the Fifth Week of Lent

We begin our prayer:
In the name of the Father, and of the Son, and of the Holy
Spirit. Amen.

O God, by whose wondrous grace
we are enriched with every blessing,
grant us so to pass from former ways to newness of life,
that we may be made ready for the glory of the heavenly
    Kingdom.
Through our Lord Jesus Christ, your Son,
who lives and reigns with you in the unity of the Holy Spirit,
one God, for ever and ever.

Collect, Monday of the Fifth Week of Lent

Reading (*Lectio*)

Read the following Scripture two or three times.

John 12:20-33

Some Greeks who had come to worship at the
Passover Feast came to Philip, who was from
Bethsaida in Galilee, and asked him, "Sir, we would
like to see Jesus." Philip went and told Andrew;
then Andrew and Philip went and told Jesus. Jesus
answered them, "The hour has come for the Son of
Man to be glorified. Amen, amen, I say to you, unless a

grain of wheat falls to the ground and dies, it remains just a grain of wheat; but if it dies, it produces much fruit. Whoever loves his life loses it, and whoever hates his life in this world will preserve it for eternal life. Whoever serves me must follow me, and where I am, there also will my servant be. The Father will honor whoever serves me.

"I am troubled now. Yet what should I say? 'Father, save me from this hour'? But it was for this purpose that I came to this hour. Father, glorify your name." Then a voice came from heaven, "I have glorified it and will glorify it again." The crowd there heard it and said it was thunder; but others said, "An angel has spoken to him." Jesus answered and said, "This voice did not come for my sake but for yours. Now is the time of judgment on this world; now the ruler of this world will be driven out. And when I am lifted up from the earth, I will draw everyone to myself." He said this indicating the kind of death he would die.

Meditation (*Meditatio*)

After the reading, take some time to reflect in silence on one or more of the following questions:

- What word or words in this passage caught your attention?
- What in this passage comforted you?
- What in this passage challenged you?

If practicing lectio divina *as a family or in a group, after the reflection time, invite the participants to share their responses.*

Prayer (*Oratio*)

Read the scripture passage one more time. Bring to the Lord the praise, petition, or thanksgiving that the Word inspires in you.

Contemplation (*Contemplatio*)

Read the Scripture again, followed by this reflection:

 What conversion of mind, heart, and life is the Lord asking of me?

 "Sir, we would like to see Jesus." Where do I see the hand of God working in my life? How can I help others to perceive the presence of God?

 Unless a grain of wheat falls to the ground and dies, it remains just a grain of wheat; but if it dies, it produces much fruit. In what ways do I need to die to myself? What fruit can my life bear for God?

Whoever serves me must follow me. How can I serve God and his Church? How can I follow God more closely?

After a period of silent reflection and/or discussion, all recite the Lord's Prayer and the following:

Closing Prayer

Have mercy on me, O God, in your goodness;
    in the greatness of your compassion wipe out my offense.
Thoroughly wash me from my guilt
    and of my sin cleanse me.

A clean heart create for me, O God,
    and a steadfast spirit renew within me.
Cast me not out from your presence,
    and your Holy Spirit take not from me.

Give me back the joy of your salvation,
    and a willing spirit sustain in me.
I will teach transgressors your ways,
    and sinners shall return to you.

From Psalm 51

Living the Word This Week

How can I make my life a gift for others in charity?

Research your parish or diocesan evangelization efforts and identify a way that you can participate.

MARCH 28, 2021

Lectio Divina for Holy Week

We begin our prayer:
In the name of the Father, and of the Son, and of the Holy Spirit. Amen.

May your mercy, O God,
cleanse the people that are subject to you
from all seduction of former ways
and make them capable of new holiness.
Through Christ our Lord.

Prayer over the People, Tuesday of Holy Week

Reading (*Lectio*)

Read the following Scripture two or three times.

Mark 11:1-10

When Jesus and his disciples drew near to Jerusalem, to Bethphage and Bethany at the Mount of Olives, he sent two of his disciples and said to them, "Go into the village opposite you, and immediately on entering it, you will find a colt tethered on which no one has ever sat. Untie it and bring it here. If anyone should say to you, 'Why are you doing this?' reply, 'The Master has need of it and will send it back here at once.'" So they went off and found a colt tethered at a gate outside on the street, and they untied it. Some of the bystanders said to them, "What are you doing, untying the colt?" They answered them just as Jesus had told them to, and

they permitted them to do it. So they brought the colt to Jesus and put their cloaks over it. And he sat on it. Many people spread their cloaks on the road, and others spread leafy branches that they had cut from the fields. Those preceding him as well as those following kept crying out:
"Hosanna!

Blessed is he who comes in the name of the Lord!

Blessed is the kingdom of our father David that is to come!

Hosanna in the highest!"

Meditation (*Meditatio*)

After the reading, take some time to reflect in silence on one or more of the following questions:

- What word or words in this passage caught your attention?
- What in this passage comforted you?
- What in this passage challenged you?

If practicing lectio divina *as a family or in a group, after the reflection time, invite the participants to share their responses.*

Prayer (*Oratio*)

Read the scripture passage one more time. Bring to the Lord the praise, petition, or thanksgiving that the Word inspires in you.

Contemplation (*Contemplatio*)

Read the Scripture again, followed by this reflection:

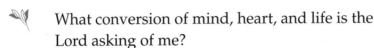 What conversion of mind, heart, and life is the Lord asking of me?

Jesus and his disciples drew near to Jerusalem. How can I draw near to Jesus in these final days of Lent? How can I maintain this nearness once Lent is over?

The Master has need of it and will send it back here at once. How can I express gratitude for the gifts that God has given me? How can I place my gifts in the Lord's service?

Blessed is the kingdom of our father David that is to come! How can I help to build God's kingdom? How can I learn to long for the coming of God's kingdom?

After a period of silent reflection and/or discussion, all recite the Lord's Prayer and the following:

Closing Prayer

All who see me scoff at me;
    they mock me with parted lips, they wag their heads:
"He relied on the LORD; let him deliver him,
    let him rescue him, if he loves him."

Indeed, many dogs surround me,
    a pack of evildoers closes in upon me;
They have pierced my hands and my feet;
    I can count all my bones.

They divide my garments among them,
    and for my vesture they cast lots.
But you, O LORD, be not far from me;
    O my help, hasten to aid me.

I will proclaim your name to my brethren;
  in the midst of the assembly I will praise you:
"You who fear the Lord, praise him;
  all you descendants of Jacob, give glory to him;
  revere him, all you descendants of Israel!"

From Psalm 22

Living the Word This Week

How can I make my life a gift for others in charity?

As much as possible, participate in your parish's celebration of
the Paschal Triduum.

April 4, 2021

Lectio Divina for the Octave of Easter

We begin our prayer:
In the name of the Father, and of the Son, and of the Holy
Spirit. Amen.

Almighty ever-living God,
who gave us the Paschal Mystery
in the covenant you established
for reconciling the human race,
so dispose our minds, we pray,
that what we celebrate by professing the faith
we may express in deeds.
Through our Lord Jesus Christ, your Son,
who lives and reigns with you in the unity of the Holy Spirit,
one God, for ever and ever.

Collect, Friday within the Octave of Easter

Reading (*Lectio*)

Read the following Scripture two or three times.

John 20:1-9

On the first day of the week, Mary of Magdala
came to the tomb early in the morning, while it
was still dark, and saw the stone removed from the
tomb. So she ran and went to Simon Peter and to the
other disciple whom Jesus loved, and told them, "They

have taken the Lord from the tomb, and we don't know where they put him." So Peter and the other disciple went out and came to the tomb. They both ran, but the other disciple ran faster than Peter and arrived at the tomb first; he bent down and saw the burial cloths there, but did not go in.

When Simon Peter arrived after him, he went into the tomb and saw the burial cloths there, and the cloth that had covered his head, not with the burial cloths but rolled up in a separate place. Then the other disciple also went in, the one who had arrived at the tomb first, and he saw and believed. For they did not yet understand the Scripture that he had to rise from the dead.

Meditation (*Meditatio*)

After the reading, take some time to reflect in silence on one or more of the following questions:

- What word or words in this passage caught your attention?
- What in this passage comforted you?
- What in this passage challenged you?

If practicing lectio divina *as a family or in a group, after the reflection time, invite the participants to share their responses.*

Prayer (*Oratio*)

Read the scripture passage one more time. Bring to the Lord the praise, petition, or thanksgiving that the Word inspires in you.

Contemplation (*Contemplatio*)

Read the Scripture again, followed by this reflection:

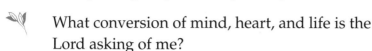 What conversion of mind, heart, and life is the Lord asking of me?

Mary of Magdala came to the tomb early in the morning, while it was still dark. When have I experienced darkness in my faith and hope? How can I share the light of Christ with others?

He saw and believed. What people, events, or books have helped me to believe more fervently? How do my words and actions help others to believe?

For they did not yet understand the Scripture that he had to rise from the dead. How often do I read Scripture and pray with it? What resources will help me grow in my understanding of the faith?

After a period of silent reflection and/or discussion, all recite the Lord's Prayer and the following:

Closing Prayer

Give thanks to the LORD, for he is good,
    for his mercy endures forever.
Let the house of Israel say,
    "His mercy endures forever."

"The right hand of the LORD has struck with power;
    the right hand of the LORD is exalted.
I shall not die, but live,
    and declare the works of the LORD."

The stone which the builders rejected
    has become the cornerstone.
By the LORD has this been done;
    it is wonderful in our eyes.

From Psalm 118

Living the Word This Week

How can I make my life a gift for others in charity?

Join or start a bible study in your parish.

APRIL 11, 2021

Lectio Divina for the Second Week of Easter

We begin our prayer:
In the name of the Father, and of the Son, and of the Holy
Spirit. Amen.

O God, who willed that through the paschal mysteries
the gates of mercy should stand open for your faithful,
look upon us and have mercy,
that as we follow, by your gift, the way you desire for us,
so may we never stray from the paths of life.
Through our Lord Jesus Christ, your Son,
who lives and reigns with you in the unity of the Holy Spirit,
one God, for ever and ever.

Collect, Saturday of the Second Week of Easter

Reading (*Lectio*)

Read the following Scripture two or three times.

John 20:19-31

On the evening of that first day of the week, when
the doors were locked, where the disciples were,
for fear of the Jews, Jesus came and stood in their
midst and said to them, "Peace be with you." When he
had said this, he showed them his hands and his side.
The disciples rejoiced when they saw the Lord. Jesus
said to them again, "Peace be with you. As the Father

has sent me, so I send you." And when he had said this, he breathed on them and said to them, "Receive the Holy Spirit. Whose sins you forgive are forgiven them, and whose sins you retain are retained."

Thomas, called Didymus, one of the Twelve, was not with them when Jesus came. So the other disciples said to him, "We have seen the Lord." But he said to them, "Unless I see the mark of the nails in his hands and put my finger into the nailmarks and put my hand into his side, I will not believe."

Now a week later his disciples were again inside and Thomas was with them. Jesus came, although the doors were locked, and stood in their midst and said, "Peace be with you." Then he said to Thomas, "Put your finger here and see my hands, and bring your hand and put it into my side, and do not be unbelieving, but believe." Thomas answered and said to him, "My Lord and my God!" Jesus said to him, "Have you come to believe because you have seen me? Blessed are those who have not seen and have believed."

Now Jesus did many other signs in the presence of his disciples that are not written in this book. But these are written that you may come to believe that Jesus is the Christ, the Son of God, and that through this belief you may have life in his name.

Meditation (*Meditatio*)

After the reading, take some time to reflect in silence on one or more of the following questions:

- What word or words in this passage caught your attention?
- What in this passage comforted you?
- What in this passage challenged you?

If practicing lectio divina *as a family or in a group, after the reflection time, invite the participants to share their responses.*

Prayer (*Oratio*)

Read the scripture passage one more time. Bring to the Lord the praise, petition, or thanksgiving that the Word inspires in you.

Contemplation (*Contemplatio*)

Read the Scripture again, followed by this reflection:

 What conversion of mind, heart, and life is the Lord asking of me?

 The doors were locked. When do I keep my faith locked inside me instead of sharing it? When have my words and actions pushed people away from God?

Peace be with you. What parts of my life (home, work, etc.) are in turmoil? How can I be a peacemaker in my environment?

But these are written that you may come to believe that Jesus is the Christ, the Son of God. What experiences bring me closer to God? How can I share these experiences with others?

After a period of silent reflection and/or discussion, all recite the Lord's Prayer and the following:

Closing Prayer

Let the house of Israel say,
  "His mercy endures forever."
Let the house of Aaron say,
  "His mercy endures forever."
Let those who fear the LORD say,
  "His mercy endures forever."
I was hard pressed and was falling,
  but the LORD helped me.

My strength and my courage is the LORD,
and he has been my savior.
The joyful shout of victory
in the tents of the just:

The stone which the builders rejected
has become the cornerstone.
By the LORD has this been done;
it is wonderful in our eyes.
This is the day the LORD has made;
let us be glad and rejoice in it.

From Psalm 118

Living the Word This Week

How can I make my life a gift for others in charity?

Join your diocesan peace and justice advocacy network and/
or pray for those who work to bring peace to places in turmoil.

April 18, 2021

Lectio Divina for the Third Week of Easter

We begin our prayer:
In the name of the Father, and of the Son, and of the Holy Spirit. Amen.

Almighty ever-living God,
let us feel your compassion more readily
during these days when, by your gift,
we have known it more fully,
so that those you have freed from the darkness of error
may cling more firmly to the teachings of your truth.
Through our Lord Jesus Christ, your Son,
who lives and reigns with you in the unity of the Holy Spirit,
one God, for ever and ever.

Collect, Thursday of the Third Week of Easter

Reading (*Lectio*)

Read the following Scripture two or three times.

Luke 24:35-48

The two disciples recounted what had taken place on the way, and how Jesus was made known to them in the breaking of bread.

While they were still speaking about this, he stood in their midst and said to them, "Peace be with you."

But they were startled and terrified and thought that they were seeing a ghost. Then he said to them, "Why are you troubled? And why do questions arise in your hearts?

Look at my hands and my feet, that it is I myself. Touch me and see, because a ghost does not have flesh and bones as you can see I have." And as he said this, he showed them his hands and his feet. While they were still incredulous for joy and were amazed, he asked them, "Have you anything here to eat?" They gave him a piece of baked fish; he took it and ate it in front of them.

He said to them, "These are my words that I spoke to you while I was still with you, that everything written about me in the law of Moses and in the prophets and psalms must be fulfilled." Then he opened their minds to understand the Scriptures. And he said to them, "Thus it is written that the Christ would suffer and rise from the dead on the third day and that repentance, for the forgiveness of sins, would be preached in his name to all the nations, beginning from Jerusalem. You are witnesses of these things."

Meditation (*Meditatio*)

After the reading, take some time to reflect in silence on one or more of the following questions:

- What word or words in this passage caught your attention?
- What in this passage comforted you?
- What in this passage challenged you?

If practicing lectio divina *as a family or in a group, after the reflection time, invite the participants to share their responses.*

Prayer (*Oratio*)

Read the scripture passage one more time. Bring to the Lord the praise, petition, or thanksgiving that the Word inspires in you.

Contemplation (*Contemplatio*)

Read the Scripture again, followed by this reflection:

 What conversion of mind, heart, and life is the Lord asking of me?

 Jesus was made known to them in the breaking of bread. How can I make the Eucharistic liturgy more central in my life? Where do I see Jesus acting in my life?

And why do questions arise in your hearts? What issues or circumstances raise questions or doubts in my heart? What resources are available to me to respond to these questions or doubts?

You are witnesses of these things. Whose witness has strengthened my faith? To whom have I given witness of my faith?

After a period of silent reflection and/or discussion, all recite the Lord's Prayer and the following:

Closing Prayer

When I call, answer me, O my just God,
   you who relieve me when I am in distress;
   have pity on me, and hear my prayer!

Know that the LORD does wonders for his faithful one;
   the LORD will hear me when I call upon him.

O LORD, let the light of your countenance shine upon us!
  You put gladness into my heart.

As soon as I lie down, I fall peacefully asleep,
  for you alone, O LORD,
  bring security to my dwelling.

From Psalm 4

Living the Word This Week

How can I make my life a gift for others in charity?

Attend daily Mass or spend some time praying before the Blessed Sacrament.

April 25, 2021

Lectio Divina for the Fourth Week of Easter

We begin our prayer:
In the name of the Father, and of the Son, and of the Holy
Spirit. Amen.

O God, life of the faithful,
glory of the humble, blessedness of the just,
listen kindly to the prayers
of those who call on you,
that they who thirst for what you generously promise
may always have their fill of your plenty.
Through our Lord Jesus Christ, your Son,
who lives and reigns with you in the unity of the Holy Spirit,
one God, for ever and ever.

Collect, Wednesday of the Fourth Week of Easter

Reading (*Lectio*)

Read the following Scripture two or three times.

John 10:11-18

Jesus said: "I am the good shepherd. A good
shepherd lays down his life for the sheep. A hired
man, who is not a shepherd and whose sheep are not
his own, sees a wolf coming and leaves the sheep and
runs away, and the wolf catches and scatters them.
This is because he works for pay and has no concern

for the sheep. I am the good shepherd, and I know mine and mine know me, just as the Father knows me and I know the Father; and I will lay down my life for the sheep. I have other sheep that do not belong to this fold. These also I must lead, and they will hear my voice, and there will be one flock, one shepherd. This is why the Father loves me, because I lay down my life in order to take it up again. No one takes it from me, but I lay it down on my own. I have power to lay it down, and power to take it up again. This command I have received from my Father."

Meditation (*Meditatio*)

After the reading, take some time to reflect in silence on one or more of the following questions:

- What word or words in this passage caught your attention?
- What in this passage comforted you?
- What in this passage challenged you?

If practicing lectio divina *as a family or in a group, after the reflection time, invite the participants to share their responses.*

Prayer (*Oratio*)

Read the scripture passage one more time. Bring to the Lord the praise, petition, or thanksgiving that the Word inspires in you.

Contemplation (*Contemplatio*)

Read the Scripture again, followed by this reflection:

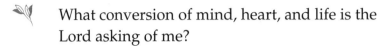 What conversion of mind, heart, and life is the Lord asking of me?

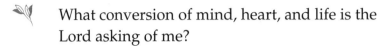 *A good shepherd lays down his life for the sheep.* Who has sacrificed for my good? How am I being called to lay down my life for others?

 I am the good shepherd, and I know mine and mine know me. How do people know that I belong to God? How can I lead those I meet to God?

The Father knows me and I know the Father. How am I growing in my knowledge of the faith? How can I come to know the Father's will for me?

After a period of silent reflection and/or discussion, all recite the Lord's Prayer and the following:

Closing Prayer

Give thanks to the LORD, for he is good,
    for his mercy endures forever.
It is better to take refuge in the LORD
    than to trust in man.
It is better to take refuge in the LORD
    than to trust in princes.

I will give thanks to you, for you have answered me
    and have been my savior.
The stone which the builders rejected
    has become the cornerstone.
By the LORD has this been done;
    it is wonderful in our eyes.

Blessed is he who comes in the name of the LORD;
    we bless you from the house of the LORD.
I will give thanks to you, for you have answered me
    and have been my savior.

Give thanks to the LORD, for he is good;
    for his kindness endures forever.

From Psalm 118

Living the Word This Week

How can I make my life a gift for others in charity?

Give up a small pleasure and donate the savings (in time or money) to those in need.

May 2, 2021

Lectio Divina for the Fifth Week of Easter

We begin our prayer:

In the name of the Father, and of the Son, and of the Holy Spirit. Amen.

O God, who restore us to eternal life
in the Resurrection of Christ,
grant your people constancy in faith and hope,
that we may never doubt the promises
of which we have learned from you.
Through our Lord Jesus Christ, your Son,
who lives and reigns with you in the unity of the Holy Spirit,
one God, for ever and ever.

Collect, Tuesday of the Fifth Week in Ordinary Time

Reading (*Lectio*)

Read the following Scripture two or three times.

John 15:1-8

Jesus said to his disciples: "I am the true vine, and my Father is the vine grower. He takes away every branch in me that does not bear fruit, and every one that does he prunes so that it bears more fruit. You are already pruned because of the word that I spoke to you. Remain in me, as I remain in you. Just as a branch cannot bear fruit on its own unless it remains on the vine, so neither can you unless you remain in me. I am the vine, you are the branches. Whoever remains in me and I in him will bear much fruit, because without me you can do nothing. Anyone who does not remain in me will be thrown out like a branch and wither; people will gather them and throw them into a fire and they will be burned. If you remain in me and my words remain in you, ask for whatever you want and it will be done for you. By this is my Father glorified, that you bear much fruit and become my disciples."

Meditation (*Meditatio*)

After the reading, take some time to reflect in silence on one or more of the following questions:

- What word or words in this passage caught your attention?
- What in this passage comforted you?
- What in this passage challenged you?

If practicing lectio divina *as a family or in a group, after the reflection time, invite the participants to share their responses.*

Prayer (*Oratio*)

Read the scripture passage one more time. Bring to the Lord the praise, petition, or thanksgiving that the Word inspires in you.

Contemplation (*Contemplatio*)

Read the Scripture again, followed by this reflection:

What conversion of mind, heart, and life is the Lord asking of me?

Every one that does he prunes so that it bears more fruit. What parts of my life need to be pruned away? What fruit has God brought to bear in my life?

Without me you can do nothing. When have I most relied on God? What is God calling me to do?

By this is my Father glorified, that you bear much fruit and become my disciples. How does my life glorify God? How can I follow the path of discipleship more closely?

After a period of silent reflection and/or discussion, all recite the Lord's Prayer and the following:

Closing Prayer

I will fulfill my vows before those who fear the LORD.
  The lowly shall eat their fill;
they who seek the LORD shall praise him:
  "May your hearts live forever!"

All the ends of the earth
  shall remember and turn to the LORD;
all the families of the nations
  shall bow down before him.

To him alone shall bow down
  all who sleep in the earth;
before him shall bend
  all who go down into the dust.

And to him my soul shall live;
  my descendants shall serve him.
Let the coming generation be told of the LORD
  that they may proclaim to a people yet to be born
  the justice he has shown.

From Psalm 22

Living the Word This Week

How can I make my life a gift for others in charity?

Review your stewardship commitments of time, talent and treasure to share in gratitude the fruit that God has brought to bear in your life.

MAY 9, 2021

Lectio Divina for the Sixth Week of Easter

We begin our prayer:
In the name of the Father, and of the Son, and of the Holy
Spirit. Amen.

O God, who made your people
partakers in your redemption,
grant, we pray,
that we may perpetually render thanks
for the Resurrection of the Lord.
Who lives and reigns with you in the unity of the Holy Spirit,
one God, for ever and ever.

Collect, Thursday of the Sixth Week of Easter

Reading (*Lectio*)

Read the following Scripture two or three times.

John 15:9-17

Jesus said to his disciples: "As the Father loves me, so
I also love you. Remain in my love. If you keep my
commandments, you will remain in my love, just as I
have kept my Father's commandments and remain in
his love.

"I have told you this so that my joy may be in
you and your joy might be complete. This is my

commandment: love one another as I love you. No
one has greater love than this, to lay down one's life
for one's friends. You are my friends if you do what I
command you. I no longer call you slaves, because a
slave does not know what his master is doing. I have
called you friends, because I have told you everything
I have heard from my Father. It was not you who chose
me, but I who chose you and appointed you to go
and bear fruit that will remain, so that whatever you
ask the Father in my name he may give you. This I
command you: love one another."

Meditation (*Meditatio*)

After the reading, take some time to reflect in silence on one or more
of the following questions:

- What word or words in this passage caught
  your attention?
- What in this passage comforted you?
- What in this passage challenged you?

If practicing lectio divina *as a family or in a group, after the*
reflection time, invite the participants to share their responses.

Prayer (*Oratio*)

Read the scripture passage one more time. Bring to the Lord the
praise, petition, or thanksgiving that the Word inspires in you.

Contemplation (*Contemplatio*)

Read the Scripture again, followed by this reflection:

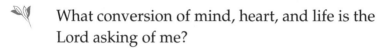 What conversion of mind, heart, and life is the Lord asking of me?

Remain in my love. When have I felt God's love most strongly? What things separate me from God's love?

I have told you this so that my joy may be in you and your joy might be complete. What do I need to complete my joy? How can I share the joy that God gives me?

It was not you who chose me, but I who chose you. What has God chosen me to do? How can I participate more fully in the mission of the Church?

After a period of silent reflection and/or discussion, all recite the Lord's Prayer and the following:

Closing Prayer

Sing to the LORD a new song,
 for he has done wondrous deeds;
His right hand has won victory for him,
 his holy arm.

The LORD has made his salvation known:
 in the sight of the nations he has revealed his justice.
He has remembered his kindness and his faithfulness
 toward the house of Israel.

All the ends of the earth have seen
 the salvation by our God.
Sing joyfully to the LORD, all you lands;
 break into song; sing praise.

From Psalm 98

Living the Word This Week

How can I make my life a gift for others in charity?

Read and reflect on "The Mysterious Working of the Risen Christ and His Spirit," paragraphs 275-280 of Pope Francis's Apostolic Exhortation *The Joy of the Gospel: http://w2.vatican.va/content/francesco/en/apost_exhortations/documents/papa-francesco_esortazione-ap_20131124_evangelii-gaudium.html.*

MAY 13, 2021

Lectio Divina for the Solemnity of the Ascension

We begin our prayer:
In the name of the Father, and of the Son, and of the Holy Spirit. Amen.

O God, whose Son today ascended to the heavens
as the Apostles looked on,
grant, we pray, that, in accordance with his promise,
we may be worthy for him to live with us always on earth,
and we with him in heaven.
Who lives and reigns with you in the unity of the Holy Spirit,
one God, for ever and ever.

Collect, Ascension, Vigil Mass

Reading (*Lectio*)

Read the following Scripture two or three times.

Mark 16:15-20

Jesus said to his disciples: "Go into the whole world and proclaim the gospel to every creature. Whoever believes and is baptized will be saved; whoever does not believe will be condemned. These signs will accompany those who believe: in my name they will drive out demons, they will speak new languages. They will pick up serpents with their hands, and if they drink any deadly thing, it will not harm them. They will lay hands on the sick, and they will recover."

So then the Lord Jesus, after he spoke to them, was taken up into heaven and took his seat at the right hand of God. But they went forth and preached everywhere, while the Lord worked with them and confirmed the word through accompanying signs.

Meditation (*Meditatio*)

After the reading, take some time to reflect in silence on one or more of the following questions:

- What word or words in this passage caught your attention?
- What in this passage comforted you?
- What in this passage challenged you?

If practicing lectio divina *as a family or in a group, after the reflection time, invite the participants to share their responses.*

Prayer (*Oratio*)

Read the scripture passage one more time. Bring to the Lord the praise, petition, or thanksgiving that the Word inspires in you.

Contemplation (*Contemplatio*)

Read the Scripture again, followed by this reflection:

What conversion of mind, heart, and life is the Lord asking of me?

Go into the whole world and proclaim the gospel to every creature. When was the last time I shared my faith with someone? What opportunities for sharing my faith have I missed?

These signs will accompany those who believe. How can people tell that I am a person of faith? How does my faith shape my daily life?

But they went forth and preached everywhere. Where is God calling me to go? What holds me back from following Jesus more closely?

After a period of silent reflection and/or discussion, all recite the Lord's Prayer and the following:

Closing Prayer

All you peoples, clap your hands,
   shout to God with cries of gladness,
For the LORD, the Most High, the awesome,
   is the great king over all the earth.

God mounts his throne amid shouts of joy;
   the LORD, amid trumpet blasts.
Sing praise to God, sing praise;
   sing praise to our king, sing praise.

For king of all the earth is God;
   sing hymns of praise.
God reigns over the nations,
   God sits upon his holy throne.

From Psalm 47

Living the Word This Week

How can I make my life a gift for others in charity?

Invite a friend or neighbor to come to Mass with you for the Solemnity of Pentecost.

MAY 16, 2021

Lectio Divina for the Seventh Week of Easter

We begin our prayer:
In the name of the Father, and of the Son, and of the Holy
Spirit. Amen.

May the power of the Holy Spirit
come to us, we pray, O Lord,
that we may keep your will faithfully in mind
and express it in a devout way of life.
Through our Lord Jesus Christ, your Son,
who lives and reigns with you in the unity of the Holy Spirit,
one God, for ever and ever.

Collect, Monday of the Seventh Week of Easter

Reading (*Lectio*)

Read the following Scripture two or three times.

John 17:11b-19

Lifting up his eyes to heaven, Jesus prayed saying:
"Holy Father, keep them in your name that you
have given me, so that they may be one just as we are
one. When I was with them I protected them in your
name that you gave me, and I guarded them, and none
of them was lost except the son of destruction, in order
that the Scripture might be fulfilled. But now I am
coming to you. I speak this in the world so that they

may share my joy completely. I gave them your word, and the world hated them, because they do not belong to the world any more than I belong to the world. I do not ask that you take them out of the world but that you keep them from the evil one. They do not belong to the world any more than I belong to the world. Consecrate them in the truth. Your word is truth. As you sent me into the world, so I sent them into the world. And I consecrate myself for them, so that they also may be consecrated in truth."

Meditation (*Meditatio*)

After the reading, take some time to reflect in silence on one or more of the following questions:

- What word or words in this passage caught your attention?
- What in this passage comforted you?
- What in this passage challenged you?

If practicing lectio divina *as a family or in a group, after the reflection time, invite the participants to share their responses.*

Prayer (*Oratio*)

Read the scripture passage one more time. Bring to the Lord the praise, petition, or thanksgiving that the Word inspires in you.

Contemplation (*Contemplatio*)

Read the Scripture again, followed by this reflection:

What conversion of mind, heart, and life is the Lord asking of me?

So that they may be one just as we are one. With whom do I need to be reconciled? How have I been a force for unity or division?

I protected them in your name that you gave me. How can I show reverence for God's holy name? From what do I need God's protection?

They do not belong to the world any more than I belong to the world. How have I accepted the world's values? How have I rejected the world values?

After a period of silent reflection and/or discussion, all recite the Lord's Prayer and the following:

Closing Prayer

> Bless the LORD, O my soul;
> > and all my being, bless his holy name.
> Bless the LORD, O my soul,
> > and forget not all his benefits.
>
> For as the heavens are high above the earth,
> > so surpassing is his kindness toward those who fear him.
> As far as the east is from the west,
> > so far has he put our transgressions from us.
>
> The LORD has established his throne in heaven,
> > and his kingdom rules over all.
> Bless the LORD, all you his angels,
> > you mighty in strength, who do his bidding.

From Psalm 103

Living the Word This Week

How can I make my life a gift for others in charity?

Look for ways to become involved in your diocese's ecumenical efforts and prayer for the unity of Christ's Church.

MAY 23, 2021

Lectio Divina for the Solemnity of Pentecost

We begin our prayer:
In the name of the Father, and of the Son, and of the Holy
Spirit. Amen.

Fulfill for us your gracious promise,
O Lord, we pray, so that by his coming
the Holy Spirit may make us witnesses before the world
to the Gospel of our Lord Jesus Christ.
Who lives and reigns for ever and ever.

Prayer after the Fourth Reading, Pentecost, Extended Vigil

Reading (*Lectio*)

Read the following Scripture two or three times.

John 15:26-27; 16:12-15

Jesus said to his disciples: "When the Advocate
comes whom I will send you from the Father, the
Spirit of truth that proceeds from the Father, he will
testify to me. And you also testify, because you have
been with me from the beginning.

"I have much more to tell you, but you cannot bear it
now. But when he comes, the Spirit of truth, he will
guide you to all truth. He will not speak on his own,
but he will speak what he hears, and will declare to

you the things that are coming. He will glorify me, because he will take from what is mine and declare it to you. Everything that the Father has is mine; for this reason I told you that he will take from what is mine and declare it to you."

Meditation (*Meditatio*)

After the reading, take some time to reflect in silence on one or more of the following questions:

- What word or words in this passage caught your attention?
- What in this passage comforted you?
- What in this passage challenged you?

If practicing lectio divina *as a family or in a group, after the reflection time, invite the participants to share their responses.*

Prayer (*Oratio*)

Read the scripture passage one more time. Bring to the Lord the praise, petition, or thanksgiving that the Word inspires in you.

Contemplation (*Contemplatio*)

Read the Scripture again, followed by this reflection:

 What conversion of mind, heart, and life is the Lord asking of me?

You also testify, because you have been with me from the beginning. How has God been present in my life? How can I testify to his presence?

The Spirit of truth . . . will guide you to all truth. How can I discern what is true? What resources do I have to lead me to the truth?

Everything that the Father has is mine. What has the Father given me? How can I respond to the Father in gratitude and generosity?

After a period of silent reflection and/or discussion, all recite the Lord's Prayer and the following:

Closing Prayer

Bless the LORD, O my soul!
O LORD, my God, you are great indeed!
How manifold are your works, O LORD!
the earth is full of your creatures;

May the glory of the LORD endure forever;
may the LORD be glad in his works!
Pleasing to him be my theme;
I will be glad in the LORD.

If you take away their breath, they perish
and return to their dust.
When you send forth your spirit, they are created,
and you renew the face of the earth.

From Psalm 104

Living the Word This Week

How can I make my life a gift for others in charity?

Consider participating in a faith formation class (in person or online) this summer.

May 30, 2021

We begin our prayer:
In the name of the Father, and of the Son, and of the Holy
Spirit. Amen.

God our Father, who by sending into the world
the Word of truth and the Spirit of sanctification
made known to the human race your wondrous mystery,
grant us, we pray, that in professing the true faith,
we may acknowledge the Trinity of eternal glory
and adore your Unity, powerful in majesty.
Through our Lord Jesus Christ, your Son,
who lives and reigns with you in the unity of the Holy Spirit,
one God, for ever and ever.

Collect, Solemnity of the Most Holy Trinity

Reading (*Lectio*)

Read the following Scripture two or three times.

Matthew 28:16-20

The eleven disciples went to Galilee, to the
mountain to which Jesus had ordered them. When
they all saw him, they worshiped, but they doubted.
Then Jesus approached and said to them, "All power
in heaven and on earth has been given to me. Go,
therefore, and make disciples of all nations, baptizing

them in the name of the Father, and of the Son, and of the Holy Spirit, teaching them to observe all that I have commanded you. And behold, I am with you always, until the end of the age."

Meditation (*Meditatio*)

After the reading, take some time to reflect in silence on one or more of the following questions:

- What word or words in this passage caught your attention?
- What in this passage comforted you?
- What in this passage challenged you?

If practicing lectio divina *as a family or in a group, after the reflection time, invite the participants to share their responses.*

Prayer (*Oratio*)

Read the scripture passage one more time. Bring to the Lord the praise, petition, or thanksgiving that the Word inspires in you.

Contemplation (*Contemplatio*)

Read the Scripture again, followed by this reflection:

 What conversion of mind, heart, and life is the Lord asking of me?

They worshiped, but they doubted. What things increase my doubt? What things give me hope and confidence?

Teaching them to observe all that I have commanded you. What holds me back from sharing the truths of the faith with others? How can I observe God's commandments more carefully?

And behold, I am with you always, until the end of the age. When do I most need to feel the Lord's presence? How can I help to make Christ's healing and reconciling love more present?

After a period of silent reflection and/or discussion, all recite the Lord's Prayer and the following:

Closing Prayer

Upright is the word of the LORD,
    and all his works are trustworthy.
He loves justice and right;
    of the kindness of the Lord the earth is full.

By the word of the LORD the heavens were made;
    by the breath of his mouth all their host.
For he spoke, and it was made;
    he commanded, and it stood forth.

See, the eyes of the LORD are upon those who fear him,
    upon those who hope for his kindness,
To deliver them from death
    and preserve them in spite of famine.

Our soul waits for the LORD,
    who is our help and our shield.
May your kindness, O LORD, be upon us
    who have put our hope in you.

From Psalm 33

Living the Word This Week

How can I make my life a gift for others in charity?

Renew your baptismal promises by praying the Apostles'
Creed.

June 6, 2021

Lectio Divina for the Solemnity of the Most Holy Body and Blood of Christ (*Corpus Christi*)

We begin our prayer:
In the name of the Father, and of the Son, and of the Holy Spirit. Amen.

O God, who in this wonderful Sacrament
have left us a memorial of your Passion,
grant us, we pray,
so to revere the sacred mysteries of your Body and Blood
that we may always experience in ourselves
the fruits of your redemption.
Who live and reign with God the Father
in the unity of the Holy Spirit,
one God, for ever and ever.

Collect, Solemnity of the Most Holy Body and Blood of Christ

Reading (*Lectio*)

Read the following Scripture two or three times.

Mark 14:12-16, 22-26

On the first day of the Feast of Unleavened Bread, when they sacrificed the Passover lamb, Jesus' disciples said to him, "Where do you want us to go and prepare for you to eat the Passover?" He sent two of his disciples and said to them, "Go into the city and a man will meet you, carrying a jar of water. Follow him. Wherever he enters, say to the master of the house, 'The Teacher says, "Where is my guest room where I may eat the Passover with my disciples?"' Then he will show you a large upper room furnished and ready. Make the preparations for us there."

The disciples then went off, entered the city, and found it just as he had told them; and they prepared the Passover.

While they were eating, he took bread, said the blessing, broke it, gave it to them, and said, "Take it; this is my body." Then he took a cup, gave thanks, and gave it to them, and they all drank from it. He said to them, "This is my blood of the covenant, which will be shed for many. Amen, I say to you, I shall not drink again the fruit of the vine until the day when I drink it new in the kingdom of God." Then, after singing a hymn, they went out to the Mount of Olives.

Meditation (*Meditatio*)

After the reading, take some time to reflect in silence on one or more of the following questions:

- What word or words in this passage caught your attention?
- What in this passage comforted you?
- What in this passage challenged you?

If practicing lectio divina *as a family or in a group, after the reflection time, invite the participants to share their responses.*

Prayer (*Oratio*)

Read the scripture passage one more time. Bring to the Lord the praise, petition, or thanksgiving that the Word inspires in you.

Contemplation (*Contemplatio*)

Read the Scripture again, followed by this reflection:

 What conversion of mind, heart, and life is the Lord asking of me?

 Where do you want us to go? Where is God calling me to share his love? How can I give my life to God more completely?

 Make the preparations for us there. How can I rearrange my priorities to make more time for God? How can I rearrange my priorities to make more time to serve my brothers and sisters?

"This is my body. . . . This is my blood." How can I be more reverent toward the Holy Eucharist? How can I express my gratitude for the gift of Jesus' Body and Blood?

After a period of silent reflection and/or discussion, all recite the Lord's Prayer and the following:

Closing Prayer

How shall I make a return to the LORD
    for all the good he has done for me?
The cup of salvation I will take up,
    and I will call upon the name of the LORD.

Precious in the eyes of the LORD
    is the death of his faithful ones.
I am your servant, the son of your handmaid;
    you have loosed my bonds.

To you will I offer sacrifice of thanksgiving,
    and I will call upon the name of the LORD.
My vows to the LORD I will pay
    in the presence of all his people.

From Psalm 116

Living the Word This Week

How can I make my life a gift for others in charity?

Spend some time reflecting on the gift of the Holy Eucharist and receive the Sacrament of Penance so as to receive Holy Communion worthily.

June 11, 2021

Lectio Divina for the Solemnity of the Sacred Heart

We begin our prayer:
In the name of the Father, and of the Son, and of the Holy
Spirit. Amen.

Grant, we pray, almighty God,
that we, who glory in the Heart of your beloved Son
and recall the wonders of his love for us,
may be made worthy to receive
an overflowing measure of grace
from that fount of heavenly gifts.
Through our Lord Jesus Christ, your Son,
who lives and reigns with you in the unity of the Holy Spirit,
one God, for ever and ever.

Collect, Solemnity of the Sacred Heart

Reading (*Lectio*)

Read the following Scripture two or three times.

John 19:31-37

Since it was preparation day, in order that the bodies
might not remain on the cross on the sabbath, for
the sabbath day of that week was a solemn one, the
Jews asked Pilate that their legs be broken and they
be taken down. So the soldiers came and broke the
legs of the first and then of the other one who was

crucified with Jesus. But when they came to Jesus and saw that he was already dead, they did not break his legs, but one soldier thrust his lance into his side, and immediately blood and water flowed out. An eyewitness has testified, and his testimony is true; he knows that he is speaking the truth, so that you also may come to believe. For this happened so that the scripture passage might be fulfilled:
Not a bone of it will be broken.

And again another passage says:
They will look upon him whom they have pierced.

Meditation (*Meditatio*)

After the reading, take some time to reflect in silence on one or more of the following questions:

- What word or words in this passage caught your attention?
- What in this passage comforted you?
- What in this passage challenged you?

If practicing lectio divina *as a family or in a group, after the reflection time, invite the participants to share their responses.*

Prayer (*Oratio*)

Read the scripture passage one more time. Bring to the Lord the praise, petition, or thanksgiving that the Word inspires in you.

Contemplation (*Contemplatio*)

Read the Scripture again, followed by this reflection:

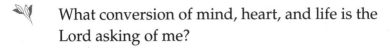 What conversion of mind, heart, and life is the Lord asking of me?

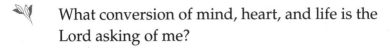 *The sabbath day of that week was a solemn one.* How do I keep holy the sabbath day? How can my faith be solemn and joy-filled?

 An eyewitness has testified, and his testimony is true. Whose testimony has helped me come to know God more fully? How can I discern what is true?

They will look upon him whom they have pierced.
How have my sins added to Jesus' burden? How
can I bear my cross more patiently?

*After a period of silent reflection and/or discussion, all recite the
Lord's Prayer and the following:*

Closing Prayer

God indeed is my savior;
    I am confident and unafraid.
My strength and my courage is the LORD,
    and he has been my savior.
With joy you will draw water
    at the fountain of salvation.

Give thanks to the LORD, acclaim his name;
    among the nations make known his deeds,
    proclaim how exalted is his name.

Sing praise to the LORD for his glorious achievement;
    let this be known throughout all the earth.
Shout with exultation, O city of Zion,
    for great in your midst
    is the Holy One of Israel!

From Isaiah 12

Living the Word This Week

How can I make my life a gift for others in charity?

Pray for the sanctity of all priests.

JUNE 13, 2021

Lectio Divina for the Eleventh Week in Ordinary Time

We begin our prayer:
In the name of the Father, and of the Son, and of the Holy
Spirit. Amen.

O God, strength of those who hope in you,
graciously hear our pleas,
and, since without you mortal frailty can do nothing,
grant us always the help of your grace,
that in following your commands
we may please you by our resolve and our deeds.
Through our Lord Jesus Christ, your Son,
who lives and reigns with you in the unity of the Holy Spirit,
one God, for ever and ever.

Collect, Eleventh Sunday in Ordinary Time

Reading (*Lectio*)

Read the following Scripture two or three times.

Mark 4:26-34

Jesus said to the crowds: "This is how it is with the
kingdom of God; it is as if a man were to scatter seed
on the land and would sleep and rise night and day
and through it all the seed would sprout and grow, he
knows not how. Of its own accord the land yields fruit,
first the blade, then the ear, then the full grain in the

ear. And when the grain is ripe, he wields the sickle at once, for the harvest has come."

He said, "To what shall we compare the kingdom of God, or what parable can we use for it? It is like a mustard seed that, when it is sown in the ground, is the smallest of all the seeds on the earth. But once it is sown, it springs up and becomes the largest of plants and puts forth large branches, so that the birds of the sky can dwell in its shade." With many such parables he spoke the word to them as they were able to understand it. Without parables he did not speak to them, but to his own disciples he explained everything in private.

Meditation (*Meditatio*)

After the reading, take some time to reflect in silence on one or more of the following questions:

- What word or words in this passage caught your attention?
- What in this passage comforted you?
- What in this passage challenged you?

If practicing lectio divina *as a family or in a group, after the reflection time, invite the participants to share their responses.*

Prayer (*Oratio*)

Read the scripture passage one more time. Bring to the Lord the praise, petition, or thanksgiving that the Word inspires in you.

Contemplation (*Contemplatio*)

Read the Scripture again, followed by this reflection:

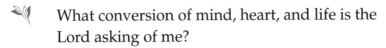 What conversion of mind, heart, and life is the Lord asking of me?

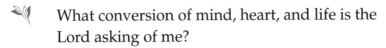 *The harvest has come.* What fruits can I bring to harvest in my life? How can these fruits serve God's kingdom?

 To what shall we compare the kingdom of God? How do I envision God's kingdom? How can I help to make the kingdom of God more present?

With many such parables he spoke the word to them as they were able to understand it. How can I share God's word more effectively? How can I grow in my understanding of all the Church teaches?

After a period of silent reflection and/or discussion, all recite the Lord's Prayer and the following:

Closing Prayer

It is good to give thanks to the LORD,
   to sing praise to your name, Most High,
To proclaim your kindness at dawn
   and your faithfulness throughout the night.

The just one shall flourish like the palm tree,
   like a cedar of Lebanon shall he grow.
They that are planted in the house of the LORD
   shall flourish in the courts of our God.

They shall bear fruit even in old age;
   vigorous and sturdy shall they be,
Declaring how just is the LORD,
   my rock, in whom there is no wrong.

From Psalm 92

Living the Word This Week

How can I make my life a gift for others in charity?

Pray one of the prayers for creation in paragraph 246 of Pope Francis's Encyclical *Laudato Si'*: *http://w2.vatican.va/content/ francesco/en/encyclicals/documents/papa-francesco_20150524_ enciclica-laudato-si.html*.

June 20, 2021

Lectio Divina for the Twelfth Week in Ordinary Time

We begin our prayer:
In the name of the Father, and of the Son, and of the Holy
Spirit. Amen.

Grant, O Lord,
that we may always revere and love your holy name,
for you never deprive of your guidance
those you set firm on the foundation of your love.
Through our Lord Jesus Christ, your Son,
who lives and reigns with you in the unity of the Holy Spirit,
one God, for ever and ever.

Collect, Twelfth Sunday in Ordinary Time

Reading (*Lectio*)

Read the following Scripture two or three times.

Mark 4:35-41

On that day, as evening drew on, Jesus said to his
disciples: "Let us cross to the other side." Leaving
the crowd, they took Jesus with them in the boat just
as he was. And other boats were with him. A violent
squall came up and waves were breaking over the
boat, so that it was already filling up. Jesus was in the
stern, asleep on a cushion. They woke him and said to
him, "Teacher, do you not care that we are perishing?"

He woke up, rebuked the wind, and said to the sea, "Quiet! Be still!" The wind ceased and there was great calm. Then he asked them, "Why are you terrified? Do you not yet have faith?" They were filled with great awe and said to one another, "Who then is this whom even wind and sea obey?"

Meditation (*Meditatio*)

After the reading, take some time to reflect in silence on one or more of the following questions:

- What word or words in this passage caught your attention?
- What in this passage comforted you?
- What in this passage challenged you?

If practicing lectio divina *as a family or in a group, after the reflection time, invite the participants to share their responses.*

Prayer (*Oratio*)

Read the scripture passage one more time. Bring to the Lord the praise, petition, or thanksgiving that the Word inspires in you.

Contemplation (*Contemplatio*)

Read the Scripture again, followed by this reflection:

What conversion of mind, heart, and life is the Lord asking of me?

Leaving the crowd, they took Jesus with them in the boat just as he was. When has the crowd pulled me away from Jesus? When have I tried to make Jesus into what I want him to be instead of who he is?

 Do you not yet have faith? When has my faith been tested? What strengthens my faith?

 They were filled with great awe. When have I been most aware of God's power and majesty? How can I show greater reverence?

After a period of silent reflection and/or discussion, all recite the Lord's Prayer and the following:

Closing Prayer

They who sailed the sea in ships,
    trading on the deep waters,
These saw the works of the LORD
    and his wonders in the abyss.

His command raised up a storm wind
    which tossed its waves on high.
They mounted up to heaven; they sank to the depths;
    their hearts melted away in their plight.

They cried to the LORD in their distress;
    from their straits he rescued them,
He hushed the storm to a gentle breeze,
    and the billows of the sea were stilled.

They rejoiced that they were calmed,
    and he brought them to their desired haven.
Let them give thanks to the LORD for his kindness
    and his wondrous deeds to the children of men.

From Psalm 107

Living the Word This Week

How can I make my life a gift for others in charity?

Spend time in silence, reflecting on the majesty and power
of God.

JUNE 27, 2021

Lectio Divina for the Thirteenth Week in Ordinary Time

We begin our prayer:
In the name of the Father, and of the Son, and of the Holy
Spirit. Amen.

O God, who through the grace of adoption
chose us to be children of light,
grant, we pray,
that we may not be wrapped in the darkness of error
but always be seen to stand in the bright light of truth.
Through our Lord Jesus Christ, your Son,
who lives and reigns with you in the unity of the Holy Spirit,
one God, for ever and ever.

Collect, Thirteenth Sunday in Ordinary Time

Reading (*Lectio*)

Read the following Scripture two or three times.

Mark 5:21-43 or 5:21-24, 35b-43

When Jesus had crossed again in the boat to the
other side, a large crowd gathered around him,
and he stayed close to the sea. One of the synagogue
officials, named Jairus, came forward. Seeing him he
fell at his feet and pleaded earnestly with him, saying,
"My daughter is at the point of death. Please, come lay
your hands on her that she may get well and live." He

went off with him, and a large crowd followed him and pressed upon him.

There was a woman afflicted with hemorrhages for twelve years. She had suffered greatly at the hands of many doctors and had spent all that she had. Yet she was not helped but only grew worse. She had heard about Jesus and came up behind him in the crowd and touched his cloak.

She said, "If I but touch his clothes, I shall be cured." Immediately her flow of blood dried up. She felt in her body that she was healed of her affliction. Jesus, aware at once that power had gone out from him, turned around in the crowd and asked, "Who has touched my clothes?" But his disciples said to Jesus, "You see how the crowd is pressing upon you, and yet you ask, 'Who touched me?'" And he looked around to see who had done it. The woman, realizing what had happened to her, approached in fear and trembling. She fell down before Jesus and told him the whole truth. He said to her, "Daughter, your faith has saved you. Go in peace and be cured of your affliction."

While he was still speaking, people from the synagogue official's house arrived and said, "Your daughter has died; why trouble the teacher any longer?" Disregarding the message that was reported, Jesus said to the synagogue official, "Do not be afraid; just have faith." He did not allow anyone to accompany him inside except Peter, James, and John, the brother of James. When they arrived at the house of the synagogue official, he caught sight of a commotion, people weeping and wailing loudly. So he went in and said to them, "Why this commotion and weeping? The child is not dead but asleep." And they ridiculed him. Then he put them all out.

He took along the child's father and mother and those who were with him and entered the room where the child was. He took the child by the hand and said to her, "*Talitha koum*," which means, "Little girl, I say to you, arise!" The girl, a child of twelve, arose immediately and walked around. At that they were utterly astounded. He gave strict orders that no one should know this and said that she should be given something to eat.

Meditation (*Meditatio*)

After the reading, take some time to reflect in silence on one or more of the following questions:

- What word or words in this passage caught your attention?
- What in this passage comforted you?
- What in this passage challenged you?

If practicing lectio divina *as a family or in a group, after the reflection time, invite the participants to share their responses.*

Prayer (*Oratio*)

Read the scripture passage one more time. Bring to the Lord the praise, petition, or thanksgiving that the Word inspires in you.

Contemplation (*Contemplatio*)

Read the Scripture again, followed by this reflection:

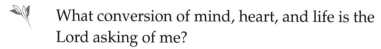 What conversion of mind, heart, and life is the Lord asking of me?

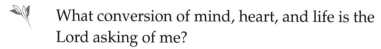 *Yet she was not helped but only grew worse.* When have I felt hopeless and in despair? How can my relationship with Jesus and his Church encourage me in such times?

 Jesus, aware at once that power had gone out from him, turned around in the crowd. When have I experienced God's power acting in my life? How can I become more aware of God acting in my life?

Do not be afraid; just have faith. What fears keep me from living by God's will? What faith practices can help me to dispel these fears?

After a period of silent reflection and/or discussion, all recite the Lord's Prayer and the following:

Closing Prayer

I will extol you, O Lord, for you drew me clear
    and did not let my enemies rejoice over me.
O Lord, you brought me up from the netherworld;
    you preserved me from among those going down into
        the pit.

Sing praise to the Lord, you his faithful ones,
    and give thanks to his holy name.
For his anger lasts but a moment;
    a lifetime, his good will.
At nightfall, weeping enters in,
    but with the dawn, rejoicing.

Hear, O Lord, and have pity on me;
    O Lord, be my helper.
You changed my mourning into dancing;
    O Lord, my God, forever will I give you thanks.

From Psalm 30

Living the Word This Week

How can I make my life a gift for others in charity?

Pray for the sick and prayerfully consider volunteering to assist with your parish's ministry to the sick and homebound.

July 4, 2021

Lectio Divina for the Fourteenth Week in Ordinary Time

We begin our prayer:
In the name of the Father, and of the Son, and of the Holy Spirit. Amen.

O God, who in the abasement of your Son
have raised up a fallen world,
fill your faithful with holy joy,
for on those you have rescued from slavery to sin
you bestow eternal gladness.
Through our Lord Jesus Christ, your Son,
who lives and reigns with you in the unity of the Holy Spirit,
one God, for ever and ever.

Collect, Fourteenth Sunday in Ordinary Time

Reading (*Lectio*)

Read the following Scripture two or three times.

Mark 6:1-6

Jesus departed from there and came to his native place, accompanied by his disciples. When the sabbath came he began to teach in the synagogue, and many who heard him were astonished. They said, "Where did this man get all this? What kind of wisdom has been given him? What mighty deeds are wrought by his hands! Is he not the carpenter, the son of Mary, and the brother of James and Joses and Judas and Simon? And are not his sisters here with us?" And they took offense at him. Jesus said to them, "A prophet is not without honor except in his native place and among his own kin and in his own house." So he was not able to perform any mighty deed there, apart from curing a few sick people by laying his hands on them. He was amazed at their lack of faith.

Meditation (*Meditatio*)

After the reading, take some time to reflect in silence on one or more of the following questions:

- What word or words in this passage caught your attention?
- What in this passage comforted you?
- What in this passage challenged you?

If practicing lectio divina *as a family or in a group, after the reflection time, invite the participants to share their responses.*

Prayer (*Oratio*)

Read the scripture passage one more time. Bring to the Lord the praise, petition, or thanksgiving that the Word inspires in you.

Contemplation (*Contemplatio*)

Read the Scripture again, followed by this reflection:

What conversion of mind, heart, and life is the Lord asking of me?

Jesus departed from there and came to his native place, accompanied by his disciples. What disciples have accompanied me on my faith journey? Who is in need of my accompaniment?

A prophet is not without honor except in his native place. When have I failed to honor those who helped to form my faith? Who are the prophets calling me to live according to God's will?

So he was not able to perform any mighty deed there. What occurrences or actions have strengthened

my faith? What deeds or actions have made me
more aware of God acting in my life?

*After a period of silent reflection and/or discussion, all recite the
Lord's Prayer and the following:*

Closing Prayer

To you I lift up my eyes
    who are enthroned in heaven—
As the eyes of servants
    are on the hands of their masters.

As the eyes of a maid
    are on the hands of her mistress,
So are our eyes on the LORD, our God,
    till he have pity on us.

Have pity on us, O LORD, have pity on us,
    for we are more than sated with contempt;
our souls are more than sated
    with the mockery of the arrogant,
    with the contempt of the proud.

From Psalm 123

Living the Word This Week

How can I make my life a gift for others in charity?

Prayerfully consider participating in the process for the Rite of Christian Initiation of Adults as a catechist or sponsor.

July 11, 2021

Lectio Divina for the Fifteenth Week in Ordinary Time

We begin our prayer:
In the name of the Father, and of the Son, and of the Holy
Spirit. Amen.

O God, who show the light of your truth
to those who go astray,
so that they may return to the right path,
give all who for the faith they profess
are accounted Christians
the grace to reject whatever is contrary to the name of Christ
and to strive after all that does it honor.
Through our Lord Jesus Christ, your Son,
who lives and reigns with you in the unity of the Holy Spirit,
one God, for ever and ever.

Collect, Fifteenth Sunday in Ordinary Time

Reading (*Lectio*)

Read the following Scripture two or three times.

Mark 6:7-13

Jesus summoned the Twelve and began to send
them out two by two and gave them authority over
unclean spirits. He instructed them to take nothing
for the journey but a walking stick— no food, no
sack, no money in their belts. They were, however,

to wear sandals but not a second tunic. He said to them, "Wherever you enter a house, stay there until you leave. Whatever place does not welcome you or listen to you, leave there and shake the dust off your feet in testimony against them." So they went off and preached repentance. The Twelve drove out many demons, and they anointed with oil many who were sick and cured them.

Meditation (*Meditatio*)

After the reading, take some time to reflect in silence on one or more of the following questions:

- What word or words in this passage caught your attention?
- What in this passage comforted you?
- What in this passage challenged you?

If practicing lectio divina *as a family or in a group, after the reflection time, invite the participants to share their responses.*

Prayer (*Oratio*)

Read the scripture passage one more time. Bring to the Lord the praise, petition, or thanksgiving that the Word inspires in you.

Contemplation (*Contemplatio*)

Read the Scripture again, followed by this reflection:

What conversion of mind, heart, and life is the Lord asking of me?

Jesus summoned the Twelve and began to send them out two by two. Where is God sending me? Who should accompany me on this journey?

He instructed them to take nothing for the journey but a walking stick. How can I be a good steward of my possessions? How can I grow in detachment from my worldly goods?

Whatever place does not welcome you or listen to you, leave there and shake the dust off your

feet in testimony against them. When have
I felt unwelcome? When have I failed to
welcome someone?

*After a period of silent reflection and/or discussion, all recite the
Lord's Prayer and the following:*

Closing Prayer

I will hear what God proclaims;
    the LORD —for he proclaims peace.
Near indeed is his salvation to those who fear him,
    glory dwelling in our land.

Kindness and truth shall meet;
    justice and peace shall kiss.
Truth shall spring out of the earth,
    and justice shall look down from heaven.

The LORD himself will give his benefits;
    our land shall yield its increase.
Justice shall walk before him,
    and prepare the way of his steps.

From Psalm 85

Living the Word This Week

How can I make my life a gift for others in charity?

Learn more about welcoming the stranger by visiting the Justice for Immigrants website: *https://justiceforimmigrants.org/.*

JULY 18, 2021

Lectio Divina for the Sixteenth Week in Ordinary Time

We begin our prayer:
In the name of the Father, and of the Son, and of the Holy
Spirit. Amen.

Show favor, O Lord, to your servants
and mercifully increase the gifts of your grace,
that, made fervent in hope, faith and charity,
they may be ever watchful in keeping your commands.
Through our Lord Jesus Christ, your Son,
who lives and reigns with you in the unity of the Holy Spirit,
one God, for ever and ever.

Collect, Sixteenth Sunday in Ordinary Time

Reading (*Lectio*)

Read the following Scripture two or three times.

Mark 6:30-34

The apostles gathered together with Jesus and
reported all they had done and taught. He said to
them, "Come away by yourselves to a deserted place
and rest a while." People were coming and going in
great numbers, and they had no opportunity even
to eat. So they went off in the boat by themselves
to a deserted place. People saw them leaving and
many came to know about it. They hastened there

on foot from all the towns and arrived at the place before them.

When he disembarked and saw the vast crowd, his heart was moved with pity for them, for they were like sheep without a shepherd; and he began to teach them many things.

Meditation (*Meditatio*)

After the reading, take some time to reflect in silence on one or more of the following questions:

- What word or words in this passage caught your attention?
- What in this passage comforted you?
- What in this passage challenged you?

If practicing lectio divina *as a family or in a group, after the reflection time, invite the participants to share their responses.*

Prayer (*Oratio*)

Read the scripture passage one more time. Bring to the Lord the praise, petition, or thanksgiving that the Word inspires in you.

Contemplation (*Contemplatio*)

Read the Scripture again, followed by this reflection:

 What conversion of mind, heart, and life is the Lord asking of me?

Come away by yourselves to a deserted place and rest a while. Where can I go to pray? How can I make space for holy leisure in my life?

They had no opportunity even to eat. How can I learn to discipline my will? What worldly concerns distract me from God?

They were like sheep without a shepherd. When have I felt lost? Who helped me find God ?

After a period of silent reflection and/or discussion, all recite the Lord's Prayer and the following:

Closing Prayer

The LORD is my shepherd; I shall not want.
    In verdant pastures he gives me repose;
beside restful waters he leads me;
    he refreshes my soul.

He guides me in right paths
    for his name's sake.
Even though I walk in the dark valley
    I fear no evil; for you are at my side
with your rod and your staff
    that give me courage.

You spread the table before me
    in the sight of my foes;
you anoint my head with oil;
    my cup overflows.

Only goodness and kindness follow me
    all the days of my life;
and I shall dwell in the house of the LORD
    for years to come.

From Psalm 23

Living the Word This Week

How can I make my life a gift for others in charity?

Fast and pray for the Holy Father's monthly prayer intention.

July 25, 2021

Lectio Divina for the Seventeenth Week in Ordinary Time

We begin our prayer:
In the name of the Father, and of the Son, and of the Holy
Spirit. Amen.

O God, protector of those who hope in you,
without whom nothing has firm foundation, nothing is holy,
bestow in abundance your mercy upon us
and grant that, with you as our ruler and guide,
we may use the good things that pass
in such a way as to hold fast even now
to those that ever endure.
Through our Lord Jesus Christ, your Son,
who lives and reigns with you in the unity of the Holy Spirit,
one God, for ever and ever.

Collect, Seventeenth Sunday in Ordinary Time

Reading (*Lectio*)

Read the following Scripture two or three times.

John 6:1-15

Jesus went across the Sea of Galilee. A large crowd
followed him, because they saw the signs he
was performing on the sick. Jesus went up on the
mountain, and there he sat down with his disciples.
The Jewish feast of Passover was near. When Jesus

raised his eyes and saw that a large crowd was coming to him, he said to Philip, "Where can we buy enough food for them to eat?" He said this to test him, because he himself knew what he was going to do. Philip answered him, "Two hundred days' wages worth of food would not be enough for each of them to have a little." One of his disciples, Andrew, the brother of Simon Peter, said to him, "There is a boy here who has five barley loaves and two fish; but what good are these for so many?" Jesus said, "Have the people recline." Now there was a great deal of grass in that place. So the men reclined, about five thousand in number. Then Jesus took the loaves, gave thanks, and distributed them to those who were reclining, and also as much of the fish as they wanted. When they had had their fill, he said to his disciples, "Gather the fragments left over, so that nothing will be wasted." So they collected them, and filled twelve wicker baskets with fragments from the five barley loaves that had been more than they could eat. When the people saw the sign he had done, they said, "This is truly the Prophet, the one who is to come into the world." Since Jesus knew that they were going to come and carry him off to make him king, he withdrew again to the mountain alone.

Meditation (*Meditatio*)

After the reading, take some time to reflect in silence on one or more of the following questions:

- What word or words in this passage caught your attention?

- What in this passage comforted you?
- What in this passage challenged you?

If practicing lectio divina *as a family or in a group, after the reflection time, invite the participants to share their responses.*

Prayer (*Oratio*)

Read the scripture passage one more time. Bring to the Lord the praise, petition, or thanksgiving that the Word inspires in you.

Contemplation (*Contemplatio*)

Read the Scripture again, followed by this reflection:

 What conversion of mind, heart, and life is the Lord asking of me?

 A large crowd followed him, because they saw the signs he was performing on the sick. Why do I follow Jesus? What do I hope to receive from him?

What good are these for so many? When have I felt that I am not doing enough? How can I address the needs I see in the world?

Gather the fragments left over, so that nothing will be wasted. What things do I tend to waste? How can I limit my waste of time, treasure, and talent?

After a period of silent reflection and/or discussion, all recite the Lord's Prayer and the following:

Closing Prayer

Let all your works give you thanks, O LORD,
    and let your faithful ones bless you.
Let them discourse of the glory of your kingdom
    and speak of your might.

The eyes of all look hopefully to you,
    and you give them their food in due season;
you open your hand
    and satisfy the desire of every living thing.

The Lord is just in all his ways
　　and holy in all his works.
The Lord is near to all who call upon him,
　　to all who call upon him in truth.

From Psalm 145

Living the Word This Week

How can I make my life a gift for others in charity?

Research food insecurity in your area and donate time, food, or money to a local food bank.

August 1, 2021

Lectio Divina for the Eighteenth Week in Ordinary Time

We begin our prayer:
In the name of the Father, and of the Son, and of the Holy
Spirit. Amen.

Draw near to your servants, O Lord,
and answer their prayers with unceasing kindness,
that, for those who glory in you as their Creator and guide,
you may restore what you have created
and keep safe what you have restored.
Through our Lord Jesus Christ, your Son,
who lives and reigns with you in the unity of the Holy Spirit,
one God, for ever and ever.

Collect, Eighteenth Sunday in Ordinary Time

Reading (*Lectio*)

Read the following Scripture two or three times.

John 6:24-35

When the crowd saw that neither Jesus nor his
disciples were there, they themselves got into
boats and came to Capernaum looking for Jesus. And
when they found him across the sea they said to him,
"Rabbi, when did you get here?" Jesus answered them
and said, "Amen, amen, I say to you, you are looking
for me not because you saw signs but because you

ate the loaves and were filled. Do not work for food that perishes but for the food that endures for eternal life, which the Son of Man will give you. For on him the Father, God, has set his seal." So they said to him, "What can we do to accomplish the works of God?" Jesus answered and said to them, "This is the work of God, that you believe in the one he sent." So they said to him, "What sign can you do, that we may see and believe in you? What can you do? Our ancestors ate manna in the desert, as it is written:
He gave them bread from heaven to eat."

So Jesus said to them, "Amen, amen, I say to you, it was not Moses who gave the bread from heaven; my Father gives you the true bread from heaven. For the bread of God is that which comes down from heaven and gives life to the world."

So they said to him, "Sir, give us this bread always." Jesus said to them, "I am the bread of life; whoever comes to me will never hunger, and whoever believes in me will never thirst."

Meditation (*Meditatio*)

After the reading, take some time to reflect in silence on one or more of the following questions:

- What word or words in this passage caught your attention?
- What in this passage comforted you?
- What in this passage challenged you?

If practicing lectio divina *as a family or in a group, after the reflection time, invite the participants to share their responses.*

Prayer (*Oratio*)

Read the scripture passage one more time. Bring to the Lord the praise, petition, or thanksgiving that the Word inspires in you.

Contemplation (*Contemplatio*)

Read the Scripture again, followed by this reflection:

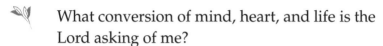 What conversion of mind, heart, and life is the Lord asking of me?

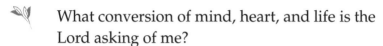 *Do not work for food that perishes.* What perishable goods occupy my time and attention? What tings should I be working for?

 What can we do to accomplish the works of God? What can I do to accomplish the works of God? How can I discern the tasks to which God is calling me?

My Father gives you the true bread from heaven.
What spiritual gifts has the Father given me?
How do I show gratitude for these gifts?

*After a period of silent reflection and/or discussion, all recite the
Lord's Prayer and the following:*

Closing Prayer

What we have heard and know,
  and what our fathers have declared to us,
We will declare to the generation to come
  the glorious deeds of the LORD and his strength
  and the wonders that he wrought.

He commanded the skies above
  and opened the doors of heaven;
he rained manna upon them for food
  and gave them heavenly bread.

Man ate the bread of angels,
  food he sent them in abundance.
And he brought them to his holy land,
  to the mountains his right hand had won.

From Psalm 78

Living the Word This Week

How can I make my life a gift for others in charity?

Keep a gratitude journal for a week and say a prayer of thanksgiving every night.

AUGUST 8, 2021

Lectio Divina for the Nineteenth Week in Ordinary Time

We begin our prayer:
In the name of the Father, and of the Son, and of the Holy
Spirit. Amen.

Almighty ever-living God,
whom, taught by the Holy Spirit,
we dare to call our Father,
bring, we pray, to perfection in our hearts
the spirit of adoption as your sons and daughters,
that we may merit to enter into the inheritance
which you have promised.
Through our Lord Jesus Christ, your Son,
who lives and reigns with you in the unity of the Holy Spirit,
one God, for ever and ever.

Collect, Nineteenth Sunday in Ordinary Time

Reading (*Lectio*)

Read the following Scripture two or three times.

John 6:41-51

The Jews murmured about Jesus because he said,
"I am the bread that came down from heaven,"
and they said, "Is this not Jesus, the son of Joseph?
Do we not know his father and mother? Then how
can he say, 'I have come down from heaven'?" Jesus

answered and said to them, "Stop murmuring among yourselves. No one can come to me unless the Father who sent me draw him, and I will raise him on the last day. It is written in the prophets:
They shall all be taught by God.

Everyone who listens to my Father and learns from him comes to me. Not that anyone has seen the Father except the one who is from God; he has seen the Father. Amen, amen, I say to you, whoever believes has eternal life. I am the bread of life. Your ancestors ate the manna in the desert, but they died; this is the bread that comes down from heaven so that one may eat it and not die. I am the living bread that came down from heaven; whoever eats this bread will live forever; and the bread that I will give is my flesh for the life of the world."

Meditation (*Meditatio*)

After the reading, take some time to reflect in silence on one or more of the following questions:

- What word or words in this passage caught your attention?
- What in this passage comforted you?
- What in this passage challenged you?

If practicing lectio divina *as a family or in a group, after the reflection time, invite the participants to share their responses.*

Prayer (*Oratio*)

Read the scripture passage one more time. Bring to the Lord the praise, petition, or thanksgiving that the Word inspires in you.

Contemplation (*Contemplatio*)

Read the Scripture again, followed by this reflection:

 What conversion of mind, heart, and life is the Lord asking of me?

 No one can come to me unless the Father who sent me draw him. How have I experienced God's call? How have I responded to that call?

 Everyone who listens to my Father and learns from him comes to me. How can I become more attentive to the Father's voice? How can I learn from him?

The bread that I will give is my flesh for the life of the world. What effects does the Eucharist have in my life? How can I give of myself for the world?

After a period of silent reflection and/or discussion, all recite the Lord's Prayer and the following:

Closing Prayer

I will bless the LORD at all times;
    his praise shall be ever in my mouth.
Let my soul glory in the LORD;
    the lowly will hear me and be glad.

Glorify the LORD with me,
    Let us together extol his name.
I sought the LORD, and he answered me
    And delivered me from all my fears.

Look to him that you may be radiant with joy.
    And your faces may not blush with shame.
When the afflicted man called out, the LORD heard,
    from all his distress he saved him.

The angel of the LORD encamps
    around those who fear him and delivers them.
Taste and see how good the LORD is;
    blessed the man who takes refuge in him.

From Psalm 34

Living the Word This Week

How can I make my life a gift for others in charity?

Spend some time in prayer before the Blessed Sacrament.

August 15, 2021

Lectio Divina for the Solemnity of the Assumption

We begin our prayer:
In the name of the Father, and of the Son, and of the Holy
Spirit. Amen.

Almighty ever-living God,
who assumed the Immaculate Virgin Mary, the Mother of
   your Son,
body and soul into heavenly glory,
grant, we pray,
that, always attentive to the things that are above,
we may merit to be sharers of her glory.
Through our Lord Jesus Christ, your Son,
who lives and reigns with you in the unity of the Holy Spirit,
one God, for ever and ever.

Collect, Solemnity of the Assumption, Mass during the Day

Reading (*Lectio*)

Read the following Scripture two or three times.

Luke 1:39-56

Mary set out and traveled to the hill country in
haste to a town of Judah, where she entered
the house of Zechariah and greeted Elizabeth. When
Elizabeth heard Mary's greeting, the infant leaped in
her womb, and Elizabeth, filled with the Holy Spirit,

cried out in a loud voice and said, "Blessed are you among women, and blessed is the fruit of your womb. And how does this happen to me, that the mother of my Lord should come to me? For at the moment the sound of your greeting reached my ears, the infant in my womb leaped for joy. Blessed are you who believed that what was spoken to you by the Lord would be fulfilled."

And Mary said:
"My soul proclaims the greatness of the Lord;
    my spirit rejoices in God my Savior
    for he has looked with favor on his lowly servant.
From this day all generations will call me blessed:
    the Almighty has done great things for me
    and holy is his Name.
    He has mercy on those who fear him
    in every generation.
He has shown the strength of his arm,
    and has scattered the proud in their conceit.
He has cast down the mighty from their thrones,
    and has lifted up the lowly.
He has filled the hungry with good things,
    and the rich he has sent away empty.
He has come to the help of his servant Israel
    for he has remembered his promise of mercy,
    the promise he made to our fathers,
    to Abraham and his children forever."

Mary remained with her about three months and then returned to her home.

Meditation (*Meditatio*)

After the reading, take some time to reflect in silence on one or more of the following questions:

- What word or words in this passage caught your attention?
- What in this passage comforted you?
- What in this passage challenged you?

If practicing lectio divina *as a family or in a group, after the reflection time, invite the participants to share their responses.*

Prayer (*Oratio*)

Read the scripture passage one more time. Bring to the Lord the praise, petition, or thanksgiving that the Word inspires in you.

Contemplation (*Contemplatio*)

Read the Scripture again, followed by this reflection:

 What conversion of mind, heart, and life is the Lord asking of me?

The infant in my womb leaped for joy. When have I responded to God with joy? How can I share the joy of the Gospel with everyone I meet?

Blessed are you who believed that what was spoken to you by the Lord would be fulfilled. When is a time that the Lord fulfilled his promise to me? How have I experienced the Lord's blessings?

He has shown the strength of his arm. How have I seen God's power working in the world? How can I be a witness to God's strength?

After a period of silent reflection and/or discussion, all recite the Lord's Prayer and the following:

Closing Prayer

The queen takes her place at your right hand in gold of
Ophir.

Hear, O daughter, and see; turn your ear,
forget your people and your father's house.

So shall the king desire your beauty;
for he is your lord.

They are borne in with gladness and joy;
they enter the palace of the king.

From Psalm 45

Living the Word This Week

How can I make my life a gift for others in charity?

Pray a decade of the Rosary (or an entire Rosary) for the needs
of the Church and the world.

AUGUST 22, 2021

Lectio Divina for the Twenty-First Week in Ordinary Time

We begin our prayer:

In the name of the Father, and of the Son, and of the Holy Spirit. Amen.

O God, who cause the minds of the faithful
to unite in a single purpose,
grant your people to love what you command
and to desire what you promise,
that, amid the uncertainties of this world,
our hearts may be fixed on that place
where true gladness is found.
Through our Lord Jesus Christ, your Son,
who lives and reigns with you in the unity of the Holy Spirit,
one God, for ever and ever.

Collect, Twenty-First Sunday in Ordinary Time

Reading (*Lectio*)

Read the following Scripture two or three times.

John 6:60-69

Many of Jesus' disciples who were listening said, "This saying is hard; who can accept it?" Since Jesus knew that his disciples were murmuring about this, he said to them, "Does this shock you?

What if you were to see the Son of Man ascending to where he was before? It is the spirit that gives life, while the flesh is of no avail. The words I have spoken to you are Spirit and life. But there are some of you who do not believe." Jesus knew from the beginning the ones who would not believe and the one who would betray him. And he said, "For this reason I have told you that no one can come to me unless it is granted him by my Father."

As a result of this, many of his disciples returned to their former way of life and no longer accompanied him. Jesus then said to the Twelve, "Do you also want to leave?" Simon Peter answered him, "Master, to whom shall we go? You have the words of eternal life. We have come to believe and are convinced that you are the Holy One of God."

Meditation (*Meditatio*)

After the reading, take some time to reflect in silence on one or more of the following questions:

- What word or words in this passage caught your attention?
- What in this passage comforted you?
- What in this passage challenged you?

If practicing lectio divina *as a family or in a group, after the reflection time, invite the participants to share their responses.*

Prayer (*Oratio*)

Read the scripture passage one more time. Bring to the Lord the praise, petition, or thanksgiving that the Word inspires in you.

Contemplation (*Contemplatio*)

Read the Scripture again, followed by this reflection:

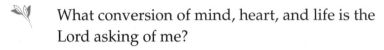 What conversion of mind, heart, and life is the Lord asking of me?

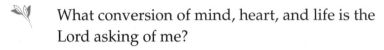 *This saying is hard; who can accept it?* What Church teachings do I struggle to accept? How can I become more docile to the Spirit?

 Many of his disciples returned to their former way of life. What are the near occasions of sin in my life? How can I remove them?

We have come to believe and are convinced that you are the Holy One of God. What strengthens my faith? How can I convince others that Jesus is the Holy One of God?

After a period of silent reflection and/or discussion, all recite the Lord's Prayer and the following:

Closing Prayer

I will bless the LORD at all times;
    his praise shall be ever in my mouth.
Let my soul glory in the LORD;
    the lowly will hear me and be glad.

The LORD has eyes for the just,
    and ears for their cry.
The LORD confronts the evildoers,
    to destroy remembrance of them from the earth.

When the just cry out, the LORD hears them,
    and from all their distress he rescues them.
The is close to the brokenhearted;
    and those who are crushed in spirit he saves.

Many are the troubles of the just one,
    but out of them all the LORD delivers him;

he watches over all his bones;
    not one of them shall be broken.

From Psalm 34

Living the Word This Week

How can I make my life a gift for others in charity?

Begin a prayerful reading of the *Catechism of the Catholic Church* or the *United States Catholic Catechism for Adults*.

August 29, 2021

Lectio Divina for the Twenty-Second Week in
Ordinary Time

We begin our prayer:
In the name of the Father, and of the Son, and of the Holy
Spirit. Amen.

God of might, giver of every good gift,
put into our hearts the love of your name,
so that, by deepening our sense of reverence,
you may nurture in us what is good
and, by your watchful care,
keep safe what you have nurtured.
Through our Lord Jesus Christ, your Son,
who lives and reigns with you in the unity of the Holy Spirit,
one God, for ever and ever.

Collect, Twenty-Second Sunday in Ordinary Time

Reading (*Lectio*)

Read the following Scripture two or three times.

Mark 7:1-8, 14-15, 21-23

When the Pharisees with some scribes who had
come from Jerusalem gathered around Jesus,
they observed that some of his disciples ate their meals
with unclean, that is, unwashed, hands.

—For the Pharisees and, in fact, all Jews, do not eat without carefully washing their hands, keeping the tradition of the elders. And on coming from the marketplace they do not eat without purifying themselves. And there are many other things that they have traditionally observed, the purification of cups and jugs and kettles and beds.— So the Pharisees and scribes questioned him, "Why do your disciples not follow the tradition of the elders but instead eat a meal with unclean hands?" He responded, "Well did Isaiah prophesy about you hypocrites, as it is written:

This people honors me with their lips,
but their hearts are far from me;
in vain do they worship me,
teaching as doctrines human precepts.

You disregard God's commandment but cling to human tradition."

He summoned the crowd again and said to them, "Hear me, all of you, and understand. Nothing that enters one from outside can defile that person; but the things that come out from within are what defile.

"From within people, from their hearts, come evil thoughts, unchastity, theft, murder, adultery, greed, malice, deceit, licentiousness, envy, blasphemy, arrogance, folly. All these evils come from within and they defile."

Meditation (*Meditatio*)

After the reading, take some time to reflect in silence on one or more of the following questions:

- What word or words in this passage caught your attention?
- What in this passage comforted you?
- What in this passage challenged you?

If practicing lectio divina *as a family or in a group, after the reflection time, invite the participants to share their responses.*

Prayer (*Oratio*)

Read the scripture passage one more time. Bring to the Lord the praise, petition, or thanksgiving that the Word inspires in you.

Contemplation (*Contemplatio*)

Read the Scripture again, followed by this reflection:

 What conversion of mind, heart, and life is the Lord asking of me?

 There are many other things that they have traditionally observed. What traditional prayers or devotions support my faith? What traditional prayers or devotions should I explore?

This people honors me with their lips, / but their hearts are far from me. When have I failed to "walk the talk" of my faith? How can I practice what I preach?

All these evils come from within and they defile. From what sin and evil must I purify my heart? How can I develop a spirit of penitence and conversion?

After a period of silent reflection and/or discussion, all recite the Lord's Prayer and the following:

Closing Prayer

Whoever walks blamelessly and does justice;
   who thinks the truth in his heart
      and slanders not with his tongue.

Who harms not his fellow man,
   nor takes up a reproach against his neighbor;

by whom the reprobate is despised,
  while he honors those who fear the LORD.

Who lends not his money at usury
  and accepts no bribe against the innocent.
Whoever does these things
  shall never be disturbed.

From Psalm 15

Living the Word This Week

How can I make my life a gift for others in charity?

Make a good examination of conscience and receive the
Sacrament of Penance.

September 5, 2021

Lectio Divina for the Twenty-Third Sunday in
Ordinary Time

We begin our prayer:
In the name of the Father, and of the Son, and of the Holy
Spirit. Amen.

O God, by whom we are redeemed and receive adoption,
look graciously upon your beloved sons and daughters,
that those who believe in Christ
may receive true freedom
and an everlasting inheritance.
Through our Lord Jesus Christ, your Son,
who lives and reigns with you in the unity of the Holy Spirit,
one God, for ever and ever.

Collect, Twenty-Third Sunday in Ordinary Time

Reading (*Lectio*)

Read the following Scripture two or three times.

Mark 7:31-37

Again Jesus left the district of Tyre and went by
way of Sidon to the Sea of Galilee, into the district
of the Decapolis. And people brought to him a deaf
man who had a speech impediment and begged him to
lay his hand on him. He took him off by himself away
from the crowd. He put his finger into the man's ears

and, spitting, touched his tongue; then he looked up to
heaven and groaned, and said to him, "*Ephphatha!*"—
that is, "Be opened!" — And immediately the man's
ears were opened, his speech impediment was
removed, and he spoke plainly. He ordered them not
to tell anyone. But the more he ordered them not to,
the more they proclaimed it. They were exceedingly
astonished and they said, "He has done all things well.
He makes the deaf hear and the mute speak."

Meditation (*Meditatio*)

*After the reading, take some time to reflect in silence on one or more
of the following questions:*

- What word or words in this passage caught
  your attention?
- What in this passage comforted you?
- What in this passage challenged you?

If practicing lectio divina *as a family or in a group, after the
reflection time, invite the participants to share their responses.*

Prayer (*Oratio*)

*Read the scripture passage one more time. Bring to the Lord the
praise, petition, or thanksgiving that the Word inspires in you.*

Contemplation (*Contemplatio*)

Read the Scripture again, followed by this reflection:

What conversion of mind, heart, and life is the Lord asking of me?

He took him off by himself away from the crowd. What distracts me from prayer? How can I eliminate these distractions?

"Ephphatha!"—that is, "Be opened!" How can I be more open to God working in my life? How can I be more open to the needs of others?

He has done all things well. What good things has God done in my life this week? How can I show my gratitude for God's goodness?

After a period of silent reflection and/or discussion, all recite the Lord's Prayer and the following:

Closing Prayer

The God of Jacob keeps faith forever,
    secures justice for the oppressed,
    gives food to the hungry.
The LORD sets captives free.

The LORD gives sight to the blind;
    the LORD raises up those who were bowed down.
The LORD loves the just;
    the LORD protects strangers.

The fatherless and the widow the LORD sustains,
    but the way of the wicked he thwarts.
The LORD shall reign forever;
    your God, O Zion, through all generations. Alleluia.

From Psalm 146

Living the Word This Week

How can I make my life a gift for others in charity?

Learn more about the Church's welcome for persons with disabilities: *http://www.usccb.org/upload/justice-persons-disabilities-bulletin-insert.pdf.*

September 12, 2021

Lectio Divina for the Twenty-Fourth Sunday in
Ordinary Time

We begin our prayer:
In the name of the Father, and of the Son, and of the Holy
Spirit. Amen.

Look upon us, O God,
Creator and ruler of all things,
and, that we may feel the working of your mercy,
grant that we may serve you with all our heart.
Through our Lord Jesus Christ, your Son,
who lives and reigns with you in the unity of the Holy Spirit,
one God, for ever and ever.

Collect, Twenty-Fourth Sunday in Ordinary Time

Reading (*Lectio*)

Read the following Scripture two or three times.

Mark 8:27-35

Jesus and his disciples set out for the villages of
Caesarea Philippi. Along the way he asked his
disciples, "Who do people say that I am?" They said in
reply, "John the Baptist, others Elijah, still others one
of the prophets." And he asked them, "But who do
you say that I am?" Peter said to him in reply, "You are
the Christ." Then he warned them not to tell anyone
about him.

He began to teach them that the Son of Man must suffer greatly and be rejected by the elders, the chief priests, and the scribes, and be killed, and rise after three days. He spoke this openly. Then Peter took him aside and began to rebuke him. At this he turned around and, looking at his disciples, rebuked Peter and said, "Get behind me, Satan. You are thinking not as God does, but as human beings do."

He summoned the crowd with his disciples and said to them, "Whoever wishes to come after me must deny himself, take up his cross, and follow me. For whoever wishes to save his life will lose it, but whoever loses his life for my sake and that of the gospel will save it."

Meditation (*Meditatio*)

After the reading, take some time to reflect in silence on one or more of the following questions:

- What word or words in this passage caught your attention?
- What in this passage comforted you?
- What in this passage challenged you?

If practicing lectio divina *as a family or in a group, after the reflection time, invite the participants to share their responses.*

Prayer (*Oratio*)

Read the scripture passage one more time. Bring to the Lord the praise, petition, or thanksgiving that the Word inspires in you.

Contemplation (*Contemplatio*)

Read the Scripture again, followed by this reflection:

❧ What conversion of mind, heart, and life is the Lord asking of me?

❧ *But who do you say that I am?* How would I describe Jesus to someone who asked me about him? How do I accompany others in their relationship with Jesus?

❧ *You are thinking not as God does, but as human beings do.* When have I made decisions based on worldly values rather than God's values? How can I learn to think with the mind of God?

Whoever wishes to come after me must deny himself, take up his cross, and follow me. What cross do I need to take up today? How can carrying this cross help me grow closer to Jesus?

After a period of silent reflection and/or discussion, all recite the Lord's Prayer and the following:

Closing Prayer

I love the LORD because he has heard
    my voice in supplication,
Because he has inclined his ear to me
    the day I called.

The cords of death encompassed me;
    the snares of the netherworld seized upon me;
    I fell into distress and sorrow,
And I called upon the name of the LORD,
    "O LORD, save my life!"

Gracious is the LORD and just;
    yes, our God is merciful.
The LORD keeps the little ones;
    I was brought low, and he saved me.

For he has freed my soul from death,
    my eyes from tears, my feet from stumbling.

I shall walk before the Lord
in the land of the living.

From Psalm 114

Living the Word This Week

How can I make my life a gift for others in charity?

Fast from food or another pleasure and offer up your sacrifice
for those persecuted for their faith.

September 14, 2021

Lectio Divina for the Feast of the Exaltation of the Holy Cross

We begin our prayer:
In the name of the Father, and of the Son, and of the Holy Spirit. Amen.

O God, who willed that your Only Begotten Son
should undergo the Cross to save the human race,
grant, we pray,
that we, who have known his mystery on earth,
may merit the grace of his redemption in heaven.
Through our Lord Jesus Christ, your Son,
who lives and reigns with you in the unity of the Holy Spirit,
one God, for ever and ever.

Collect, Feast of the Exaltation of the Holy Cross

Reading (*Lectio*)

Read the following Scripture two or three times.

John 3:13-17

Jesus said to Nicodemus: "No one has gone up to heaven except the one who has come down from heaven, the Son of Man. And just as Moses lifted up the serpent in the desert, so must the Son of Man be lifted up, so that everyone who believes in him may have eternal life."

For God so loved the world that he gave his only Son, so that everyone who believes in him might not perish but might have eternal life. For God did not send his Son into the world to condemn the world, but that the world might be saved through him.

Meditation (*Meditatio*)

After the reading, take some time to reflect in silence on one or more of the following questions:

- What word or words in this passage caught your attention?
- What in this passage comforted you?
- What in this passage challenged you?

If practicing lectio divina *as a family or in a group, after the reflection time, invite the participants to share their responses.*

Prayer (*Oratio*)

Read the scripture passage one more time. Bring to the Lord the praise, petition, or thanksgiving that the Word inspires in you.

Contemplation (*Contemplatio*)

Read the Scripture again, followed by this reflection:

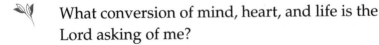 What conversion of mind, heart, and life is the Lord asking of me?

No one has gone up to heaven except the one who has come down from heaven. In what do I hope? How does my hope of heaven sustain me in life's trials?

So must the Son of Man be lifted up, so that everyone who believes in him may have eternal life. What people or experiences have "lifted up" my faith? How can I lift up the people I encounter?

For God did not send his Son into the world to condemn the world, but that the world might be saved through him. How do I condemn the world through my words or actions? How can I help to be part of the solution for the problems that I see?

After a period of silent reflection and/or discussion, all recite the Lord's Prayer and the following:

Closing Prayer

Hearken, my people, to my teaching;
    incline your ears to the words of my mouth.
I will open my mouth in a parable,
    I will utter mysteries from of old.

While he slew them they sought him
    and inquired after God again,
Remembering that God was their rock
    and the Most High God, their redeemer.

But they flattered him with their mouths
    and lied to him with their tongues,
Though their hearts were not steadfast toward him,
    nor were they faithful to his covenant.

But he, being merciful, forgave their sin
    and destroyed them not;
Often he turned back his anger
    and let none of his wrath be roused.

From Psalm 78

Living the Word This Week

How can I make my life a gift for others in charity?

Place a crucifix in a prominent place in your home and spend some time before it, praying for the needs of the world.

September 19, 2021

Lectio Divina for the Twenty-Fifth Sunday in
Ordinary Time

We begin our prayer:
In the name of the Father, and of the Son, and of the Holy
Spirit. Amen.

O God, who founded all the commands of your sacred Law
upon love of you and of our neighbor,
grant that, by keeping your precepts,
we may merit to attain eternal life.
Through our Lord Jesus Christ, your Son,
who lives and reigns with you in the unity of the Holy Spirit,
one God, for ever and ever.

Collect, Twenty-Fifth Sunday in Ordinary Time

Reading (*Lectio*)

Read the following Scripture two or three times.

Mark 9:30-37

Jesus and his disciples left from there and began a
journey through Galilee, but he did not wish anyone
to know about it. He was teaching his disciples and
telling them, "The Son of Man is to be handed over
to men and they will kill him, and three days after
his death the Son of Man will rise." But they did
not understand the saying, and they were afraid to
question him.

They came to Capernaum and, once inside the house, he began to ask them, "What were you arguing about on the way?" But they remained silent. They had been discussing among themselves on the way who was the greatest. Then he sat down, called the Twelve, and said to them, "If anyone wishes to be first, he shall be the last of all and the servant of all." Taking a child, he placed it in the their midst, and putting his arms around it, he said to them, "Whoever receives one child such as this in my name, receives me; and whoever receives me, receives not me but the One who sent me."

Meditation (*Meditatio*)

After the reading, take some time to reflect in silence on one or more of the following questions:

- What word or words in this passage caught your attention?
- What in this passage comforted you?
- What in this passage challenged you?

If practicing lectio divina *as a family or in a group, after the reflection time, invite the participants to share their responses.*

Prayer (*Oratio*)

Read the scripture passage one more time. Bring to the Lord the praise, petition, or thanksgiving that the Word inspires in you.

Contemplation (*Contemplatio*)

Read the Scripture again, followed by this reflection:

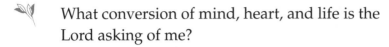 What conversion of mind, heart, and life is the Lord asking of me?

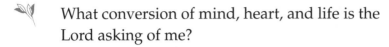 *But they did not understand the saying, and they were afraid to question him.* What questions am I afraid to ask? To whom can I entrust my faith questions?

 If anyone wishes to be first, he shall be the last of all and the servant of all. How have I been selfish this week? How can I serve my brothers and sisters?

Whoever receives me, receives not me but the One who sent me. Whom have I failed to welcome? How can I open my heart and life to those who need me?

After a period of silent reflection and/or discussion, all recite the Lord's Prayer and the following:

Closing Prayer

O God, by your name save me,
    and by your might defend my cause.
O God, hear my prayer;
    hearken to the words of my mouth.

For the haughty men have risen up against me,
    the ruthless seek my life;
    they set not God before their eyes.

Behold, God is my helper;
    the Lord sustains my life.
Freely will I offer you sacrifice;
    I will praise your name, O LORD, for its goodness.

From Psalm 54

Living the Word This Week

How can I make my life a gift for others in charity?

Learn more about providing safe environments for children and young people (*https://www.usccb.org/offices/child-and-youth-protection/ten-points-create-safe-environments-children*) and pray the Rosary for Healing and Protection: *http://www.usccb.org/issues-and-action/child-and-youth-protection/upload/Rosary-for-Healing-Printable.pdf.*

September 26, 2021

Lectio Divina for the Twenty-Sixth Sunday in
Ordinary Time

We begin our prayer:
In the name of the Father, and of the Son, and of the Holy
Spirit. Amen.

O God, who manifest your almighty power
above all by pardoning and showing mercy,
bestow, we pray, your grace abundantly upon us
and make those hastening to attain your promises
heirs to the treasures of heaven.
Through our Lord Jesus Christ, your Son,
who lives and reigns with you in the unity of the Holy Spirit,
one God, for ever and ever.

Collect, Twenty-Sixth Sunday in Ordinary Time

Reading (*Lectio*)

Read the following Scripture two or three times.

Mark 9:38-43, 45, 47-48

A t that time, John said to Jesus, "Teacher, we saw
someone driving out demons in your name, and
we tried to prevent him because he does not follow
us." Jesus replied, "Do not prevent him. There is no
one who performs a mighty deed in my name who can
at the same time speak ill of me. For whoever is not

against us is for us. Anyone who gives you a cup of water to drink because you belong to Christ, amen, I say to you, will surely not lose his reward.

"Whoever causes one of these little ones who believe in me to sin, it would be better for him if a great millstone were put around his neck and he were thrown into the sea. If your hand causes you to sin, cut it off. It is better for you to enter into life maimed than with two hands to go into Gehenna, into the unquenchable fire. And if your foot causes you to sin, cut if off. It is better for you to enter into life crippled than with two feet to be thrown into Gehenna. And if your eye causes you to sin, pluck it out. Better for you to enter into the kingdom of God with one eye than with two eyes to be thrown into Gehenna, where 'their worm does not die, and the fire is not quenched.'"

Meditation (*Meditatio*)

After the reading, take some time to reflect in silence on one or more of the following questions:

- What word or words in this passage caught your attention?
- What in this passage comforted you?
- What in this passage challenged you?

If practicing lectio divina *as a family or in a group, after the reflection time, invite the participants to share their responses.*

Prayer (*Oratio*)

Read the scripture passage one more time. Bring to the Lord the praise, petition, or thanksgiving that the Word inspires in you.

Contemplation (*Contemplatio*)

Read the Scripture again, followed by this reflection:

 What conversion of mind, heart, and life is the Lord asking of me?

 We tried to prevent him because he does not follow us. When have my words or actions prevented someone from following Jesus? In what ways have I harmed the unity in my family or in my church?

 For whoever is not against us is for us. How can I fight prejudice in my own heart and mind? In my community?

Whoever causes one of these little ones who believe in me to sin. When have I been a near occasion of sin for others? How can I be a better example, especially for those who are young or new to the faith?

After a period of silent reflection and/or discussion, all recite the Lord's Prayer and the following:

Closing Prayer

The law of the LORD is perfect,
    refreshing the soul;
the decree of the LORD is trustworthy,
    giving wisdom to the simple.

The fear of the LORD is pure,
    enduring forever;
the ordinances of the LORD are true,
    all of them just.

Though your servant is careful of them,
    very diligent in keeping them,
Yet who can detect failings?
    Cleanse me from my unknown faults!

From wanton sin especially, restrain your servant;
    let it not rule over me.

Then shall I be blameless and innocent
of serious sin.

From Psalm 19

Living the Word This Week

How can I make my life a gift for others in charity?

Consider how you can support the Church's mission through the Catholic Home Missions Appeal or support for the Pontifical Mission Societies.

October 3, 2021

Lectio Divina for the Twenty-Seventh Sunday in Ordinary Time

We begin our prayer:
In the name of the Father, and of the Son, and of the Holy Spirit. Amen.

Almighty ever-living God,
who in the abundance of your kindness
surpass the merits and the desires of those who entreat you,
pour out your mercy upon us
to pardon what conscience dreads
and to give what prayer does not dare to ask.
Through our Lord Jesus Christ, your Son,
who lives and reigns with you in the unity of the Holy Spirit,
one God, for ever and ever.

Collect, Twenty-Seventh Sunday in Ordinary Time

Reading (*Lectio*)

Read the following Scripture two or three times.

Mark 10:2-16

The Pharisees approached Jesus and asked, "Is it lawful for a husband to divorce his wife?" They were testing him. He said to them in reply, "What did Moses command you?" They replied, "Moses permitted a husband to write a bill of divorce and dismiss her." But Jesus told them, "Because of the hardness of your hearts he wrote you this commandment. But from the beginning of creation, *God made them male and female. For this reason a man shall leave his father and mother and be joined to his wife, and the two shall become one flesh.* So they are no longer two but one flesh. Therefore what God has joined together, no human being must separate." In the house the disciples again questioned Jesus about this. He said to them, "Whoever divorces his wife and marries another commits adultery against her; and if she divorces her husband and marries another, she commits adultery."

And people were bringing children to him that he might touch them, but the disciples rebuked them. When Jesus saw this he became indignant and said to them, "Let the children come to me; do not prevent them, for the kingdom of God belongs to such as these. Amen, I say to you, whoever does not accept the kingdom of God like a child will not enter it." Then he embraced them and blessed them, placing his hands on them.

Meditation (*Meditatio*)

After the reading, take some time to reflect in silence on one or more of the following questions:

- What word or words in this passage caught your attention?
- What in this passage comforted you?
- What in this passage challenged you?

If practicing lectio divina *as a family or in a group, after the reflection time, invite the participants to share their responses.*

Prayer (*Oratio*)

Read the scripture passage one more time. Bring to the Lord the praise, petition, or thanksgiving that the Word inspires in you.

Contemplation (*Contemplatio*)

Read the Scripture again, followed by this reflection:

 What conversion of mind, heart, and life is the Lord asking of me?

 Because of the hardness of your hearts he wrote you this commandment. When have I hardened my heart to God's love? How can I soften my heart and be more docile to God's commandments?

 Therefore what God has joined together, no human being must separate. When have I been an instrument of division? When have I been an instrument of unity?

Whoever does not accept the kingdom of God like a child will not enter it. What does it mean to accept the kingdom of God like a child? How can I be more childlike in my response to God's love?

After a period of silent reflection and/or discussion, all recite the Lord's Prayer and the following:

Closing Prayer

Blessed are you who fear the LORD,
    who walk in his ways!
For you shall eat the fruit of your handiwork;
    blessed shall you be, and favored.

Your wife shall be like a fruitful vine
    in the recesses of your home;
your children like olive plants
    around your table.

Behold, thus is the man blessed
    who fears the LORD.
The LORD bless you from Zion:
    may you see the prosperity of Jerusalem
    all the days of your life.

May you see your children's children.
    Peace be upon Israel!

From Psalm 128

Living the Word This Week

How can I make my life a gift for others in charity?

Prayerfully consider ways to support your parish's ministry to married couples and to those preparing for marriage.

October 10, 2021

Lectio Divina for the Twenty-Eighth Sunday in
Ordinary Time

We begin our prayer:
In the name of the Father, and of the Son, and of the Holy
Spirit. Amen.

May your grace, O Lord, we pray,
at all times go before us and follow after
and make us always determined
to carry out good works.
Through our Lord Jesus Christ, your Son,
who lives and reigns with you in the unity of the Holy Spirit,
one God, for ever and ever.

Collect, Twenty-Eighth Sunday in Ordinary Time

Reading (*Lectio*)

Read the following Scripture two or three times.

Mark 10:17-30

As Jesus was setting out on a journey, a man ran up,
knelt down before him, and asked him, "Good
teacher, what must I do to inherit eternal life?" Jesus
answered him, "Why do you call me good? No one is
good but God alone. You know the commandments:
*You shall not kill; you shall not commit adultery; you shall
not steal; you shall not bear false witness; you shall not*

defraud; honor your father and your mother." He replied and said to him, "Teacher, all of these I have observed from my youth." Jesus, looking at him, loved him and said to him, "You are lacking in one thing. Go, sell what you have, and give to the poor and you will have treasure in heaven; then come, follow me." At that statement his face fell, and he went away sad, for he had many possessions.

Jesus looked around and said to his disciples, "How hard it is for those who have wealth to enter the kingdom of God!" The disciples were amazed at his words. So Jesus again said to them in reply, "Children, how hard it is to enter the kingdom of God! It is easier for a camel to pass through the eye of a needle than for one who is rich to enter the kingdom of God." They were exceedingly astonished and said among themselves, "Then who can be saved?" Jesus looked at them and said, "For human beings it is impossible, but not for God. All things are possible for God." Peter began to say to him, "We have given up everything and followed you." Jesus said, "Amen, I say to you, there is no one who has given up house or brothers or sisters or mother or father or children or lands for my sake and for the sake of the gospel who will not receive a hundred times more now in this present age: houses and brothers and sisters and mothers and children and lands, with persecutions, and eternal life in the age to come."

Meditation (*Meditatio*)

After the reading, take some time to reflect in silence on one or more of the following questions:

- What word or words in this passage caught your attention?
- What in this passage comforted you?
- What in this passage challenged you?

If practicing lectio divina *as a family or in a group, after the reflection time, invite the participants to share their responses.*

Prayer (*Oratio*)

Read the scripture passage one more time. Bring to the Lord the praise, petition, or thanksgiving that the Word inspires in you.

Contemplation (*Contemplatio*)

Read the Scripture again, followed by this reflection:

 What conversion of mind, heart, and life is the Lord asking of me?

 Good teacher, what must I do to inherit eternal life? How do I come to know what Jesus teaches? What can I do this week to help me grow closer to God and to the eternal life to which God calls me?

Go, sell what you have, and give to the poor and you will have treasure in heaven; then come, follow me. What do I treasure? What do I do to help the poor and change their situation?

 How hard it is for those who have wealth to enter the kingdom of God! What obstacles keep me from embracing God's kingdom? How can I remove these obstacles?

After a period of silent reflection and/or discussion, all recite the Lord's Prayer and the following:

Closing Prayer

Teach us to number our days aright,
   that we may gain wisdom of heart.
Return, O LORD! How long?
   Have pity on your servants!

Fill us at daybreak with your kindness,
   that we may shout for joy and gladness all our days.

Make us glad, for the days when you afflicted us,
    for the years when we saw evil.

Let your work be seen by your servants
    and your glory by their children;
and may the gracious care of the LORD our God be ours;
    prosper the work of our hands for us!
    Prosper the work of our hands!

From Psalm 90

Living the Word This Week

How can I make my life a gift for others in charity?

Forego an unnecessary purchase or other expenditure and
give the money to the poor.

October 17, 2021

Lectio Divina for the Twenty-Ninth Sunday in
Ordinary Time

We begin our prayer:
In the name of the Father, and of the Son, and of the Holy
Spirit. Amen.

Almighty ever-living God,
grant that we may always conform our will to yours
and serve your majesty in sincerity of heart.
Through our Lord Jesus Christ, your Son,
who lives and reigns with you in the unity of the Holy Spirit,
one God, for ever and ever.

Collect, Twenty-Ninth Sunday in Ordinary Time

Reading (*Lectio*)

Read the following Scripture two or three times.

Mark 10:35-45

James and John, the sons of Zebedee, came to Jesus
and said to him, "Teacher, we want you to do for us
whatever we ask of you." He replied, "What do you
wish me to do for you?" They answered him, "Grant
that in your glory we may sit one at your right and the
other at your left."

Jesus said to them, "You do not know what you are
asking. Can you drink the cup that I drink or be

baptized with the baptism with which I am baptized?" They said to him, "We can." Jesus said to them, "The cup that I drink, you will drink, and with the baptism with which I am baptized, you will be baptized; but to sit at my right or at my left is not mine to give but is for those for whom it has been prepared." When the ten heard this, they became indignant at James and John. Jesus summoned them and said to them, "You know that those who are recognized as rulers over the Gentiles lord it over them, and their great ones make their authority over them felt. But it shall not be so among you. Rather, whoever wishes to be great among you will be your servant; whoever wishes to be first among you will be the slave of all. For the Son of Man did not come to be served but to serve and to give his life as a ransom for many."

Meditation (*Meditatio*)

After the reading, take some time to reflect in silence on one or more of the following questions:

- What word or words in this passage caught your attention?
- What in this passage comforted you?
- What in this passage challenged you?

If practicing lectio divina *as a family or in a group, after the reflection time, invite the participants to share their responses.*

Prayer (*Oratio*)

Read the scripture passage one more time. Bring to the Lord the praise, petition, or thanksgiving that the Word inspires in you.

Contemplation (*Contemplatio*)

Read the Scripture again, followed by this reflection:

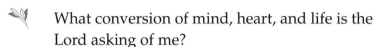 What conversion of mind, heart, and life is the Lord asking of me?

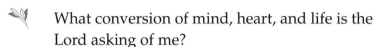 *What do you wish me to do for you?* What do I want God to do for me? What needs should I bring to God in prayer?

 The cup that I drink, you will drink. What suffering and challenges am I facing? How can I pour out my life for others?

For the Son of Man did not come to be served but to serve and to give his life as a ransom for many. What have I done this week to serve those in need? What keeps me from serving God more wholeheartedly?

After a period of silent reflection and/or discussion, all recite the Lord's Prayer and the following:

Closing Prayer

Upright is the word of the LORD,
    and all his works are trustworthy.
He loves justice and right;
    of the kindness of the LORD the earth is full.

See, the eyes of the LORD are upon those who fear him,
    upon those who hope for his kindness,
To deliver them from death
    and preserve them in spite of famine.

Our soul waits for the LORD,
    who is our help and our shield.
May your kindness, O LORD, be upon us
    who have put our hope in you.

From Psalm 33

Living the Word This Week

How can I make my life a gift for others in charity?

Pray for all deacons in their ministry of word and charity.

OCTOBER 24, 2021

Lectio Divina for the Thirtieth Sunday in Ordinary Time

We begin our prayer:
In the name of the Father, and of the Son, and of the Holy
Spirit. Amen.

Almighty ever-living God,
increase our faith, hope and charity,
and make us love what you command,
so that we may merit what you promise.
Through our Lord Jesus Christ, your Son,
who lives and reigns with you in the unity of the Holy Spirit,
one God, for ever and ever.

Collect, Thirtieth Sunday in Ordinary Time

Reading (*Lectio*)

Read the following Scripture two or three times.

Mark 10:46-52

As Jesus was leaving Jericho with his disciples and
a sizable crowd, Bartimaeus, a blind man, the son
of Timaeus, sat by the roadside begging. On hearing
that it was Jesus of Nazareth, he began to cry out and
say, "Jesus, son of David, have pity on me." And many
rebuked him, telling him to be silent. But he kept
calling out all the more, "Son of David, have pity on
me." Jesus stopped and said, "Call him." So they called

the blind man, saying to him, "Take courage; get up, Jesus is calling you." He threw aside his cloak, sprang up, and came to Jesus. Jesus said to him in reply, "What do you want me to do for you?" The blind man replied to him, "Master, I want to see." Jesus told him, "Go your way; your faith has saved you." Immediately he received his sight and followed him on the way.

Meditation (*Meditatio*)

After the reading, take some time to reflect in silence on one or more of the following questions:

- What word or words in this passage caught your attention?
- What in this passage comforted you?
- What in this passage challenged you?

If practicing lectio divina *as a family or in a group, after the reflection time, invite the participants to share their responses.*

Prayer (*Oratio*)

Read the scripture passage one more time. Bring to the Lord the praise, petition, or thanksgiving that the Word inspires in you.

Contemplation (*Contemplatio*)

Read the Scripture again, followed by this reflection:

What conversion of mind, heart, and life is the Lord asking of me?

Many rebuked him, telling him to be silent. When have I been ridiculed because of my faith? What tempts me to be silent about my faith?

He threw aside his cloak, sprang up, and came to Jesus. How have I encountered Jesus this week? What sinful attachments do I need to throw aside to follow Jesus more closely?

Immediately he received his sight and followed him on the way. How can I see things more clearly in Jesus? How can I follow Jesus more closely on the way?

After a period of silent reflection and/or discussion, all recite the Lord's Prayer and the following:

Closing Prayer

When the LORD brought back the captives of Zion,
  we were like men dreaming.
Then our mouth was filled with laughter,
  and our tongue with rejoicing.

Then they said among the nations,
  "The LORD has done great things for them."
The LORD has done great things for us;
  we are glad indeed.

Restore our fortunes, O LORD,
  like the torrents in the southern desert.
Those that sow in tears
  shall reap rejoicing.

 Although they go forth weeping,
  carrying the seed to be sown,
They shall come back rejoicing,
  carrying their sheaves.

From Psalm 126

Living the Word This Week

How can I make my life a gift for others in charity?

Plan a pilgrimage to a religious site near you and pray for
those in need as you travel.

October 31, 2021

Lectio Divina for the Thirty-First Sunday in Ordinary Time

We begin our prayer:
In the name of the Father, and of the Son, and of the Holy
Spirit. Amen.

Almighty and merciful God,
by whose gift your faithful offer you
right and praiseworthy service,
grant, we pray,
that we may hasten without stumbling
to receive the things you have promised.
Through our Lord Jesus Christ, your Son,
who lives and reigns with you in the unity of the Holy Spirit,
one God, for ever and ever.

Collect, Thirty-First Sunday in Ordinary Time

Reading (*Lectio*)

Read the following Scripture two or three times.

Mark 12:28b-34

One of the scribes came to Jesus and asked him,
"Which is the first of all the commandments?"
Jesus replied, "The first is this: *Hear, O Israel! The
Lord our God is Lord alone! You shall love the Lord your
God with all your heart, with all your soul, with all your
mind, and with all your strength. The second is this: You
shall love your neighbor as yourself. There is no other*

commandment greater than these." The scribe said to him, "Well said, teacher. You are right in saying, 'He is One and there is no other than he.' And 'to love him with all your heart, with all your understanding, with all your strength, and to love your neighbor as yourself' is worth more than all burnt offerings and sacrifices." And when Jesus saw that he answered with understanding, he said to him, "You are not far from the kingdom of God." And no one dared to ask him any more questions.

Meditation (*Meditatio*)

After the reading, take some time to reflect in silence on one or more of the following questions:

- What word or words in this passage caught your attention?
- What in this passage comforted you?
- What in this passage challenged you?

If practicing lectio divina *as a family or in a group, after the reflection time, invite the participants to share their responses.*

Prayer (*Oratio*)

Read the scripture passage one more time. Bring to the Lord the praise, petition, or thanksgiving that the Word inspires in you.

Contemplation (*Contemplatio*)

Read the Scripture again, followed by this reflection:

What conversion of mind, heart, and life is the Lord asking of me?

You shall love the Lord your God with all your heart, with all your soul, with all your mind, and with all your strength. How can I make God the top priority in my life? How can I show God my love for him this week?

You shall love your neighbor as yourself. Do I love myself as a precious child of God? Do I share God's love with those I meet?

You are not far from the kingdom of God. When have I felt close to the kingdom of God? When have I felt far from the kingdom of God?

After a period of silent reflection and/or discussion, all recite the Lord's Prayer and the following:

Closing Prayer

I love you, O LORD, my strength,
   O LORD, my rock, my fortress, my deliverer.

My God, my rock of refuge,
   my shield, the horn of my salvation, my stronghold!
Praised be the LORD, I exclaim,
   and I am safe from my enemies.

The LORD lives! And blessed be my rock!
   Extolled be God my savior.
You who gave great victories to your king
   and showed kindness to your anointed.

From Psalm 18

Living the Word This Week

How can I make my life a gift for others in charity?

Take an honest look at your schedule to find ways that you can give more time to God.

November 7, 2021

Lectio Divina for the Thirty-Second Sunday in
Ordinary Time

We begin our prayer:
In the name of the Father, and of the Son, and of the Holy
Spirit. Amen.

Almighty and merciful God,
graciously keep from us all adversity,
so that, unhindered in mind and body alike,
we may pursue in freedom of heart
the things that are yours.
Through our Lord Jesus Christ, your Son,
who lives and reigns with you in the unity of the Holy Spirit,
one God, for ever and ever.

Collect, Thirty-Second Sunday in Ordinary Time

Reading (*Lectio*)

Read the following Scripture two or three times.

Mark 12:38-44

In the course of his teaching Jesus said to the crowds,
"Beware of the scribes, who like to go around in
long robes and accept greetings in the marketplaces,
seats of honor in synagogues, and places of honor at
banquets. They devour the houses of widows and, as a
pretext recite lengthy prayers. They will receive a very
severe condemnation."

He sat down opposite the treasury and observed how the crowd put money into the treasury. Many rich people put in large sums. A poor widow also came and put in two small coins worth a few cents. Calling his disciples to himself, he said to them, "Amen, I say to you, this poor widow put in more than all the other contributors to the treasury. For they have all contributed from their surplus wealth, but she, from her poverty, has contributed all she had, her whole livelihood."

Meditation (*Meditatio*)

After the reading, take some time to reflect in silence on one or more of the following questions:

- What word or words in this passage caught your attention?
- What in this passage comforted you?
- What in this passage challenged you?

If practicing lectio divina *as a family or in a group, after the reflection time, invite the participants to share their responses.*

Prayer (*Oratio*)

Read the scripture passage one more time. Bring to the Lord the praise, petition, or thanksgiving that the Word inspires in you.

Contemplation (*Contemplatio*)

Read the Scripture again, followed by this reflection:

What conversion of mind, heart, and life is the Lord asking of me?

Beware of the scribes. What threatens my faith? How can I combat these threats?

They devour the houses of widows and, as a pretext recite lengthy prayers. When have I failed to act in justice and charity toward my brothers and sisters? How can I live my faith in greater integrity?

She, from her poverty, has contributed all she had, her whole livelihood. What can I give to God and his Church? How can I respond more generously to the needs around me?

After a period of silent reflection and/or discussion, all recite the Lord's Prayer and the following:

Closing Prayer

The Lord keeps faith forever,
    secures justice for the oppressed,
    gives food to the hungry.
The Lord sets captives free.

The Lord gives sight to the blind.
    The Lord raises up those who were bowed down;
the Lord loves the just.
    The Lord protects strangers.

The fatherless and the widow he sustains,
    but the way of the wicked he thwarts.
The Lord shall reign forever;
    your God, O Zion, through all generations. Alleluia.

From Psalm 146

Living the Word This Week

How can I make my life a gift for others in charity?

Research your parish and diocesan social justice efforts (e.g., Catholic Charities, Saint Vincent de Paul Society, Legislative Action Network, etc.) and prayerfully discern how you are called to be engaged.

November 14, 2021

Lectio Divina for the Thirty-Third Sunday in Ordinary Time

We begin our prayer:
In the name of the Father, and of the Son, and of the Holy
Spirit. Amen.

Grant us, we pray, O Lord our God,
the constant gladness of being devoted to you,
for it is full and lasting happiness
to serve with constancy
the author of all that is good.
Through our Lord Jesus Christ, your Son,
who lives and reigns with you in the unity of the Holy Spirit,
one God, for ever and ever.

Collect, Thirty-Third Sunday in Ordinary Time

Reading (*Lectio*)

Read the following Scripture two or three times.

Mark 13:24-32

Jesus said to his disciples: "In those days after that
tribulation
the sun will be darkened,
   and the moon will not give its light,
and the stars will be falling from the sky,
   and the powers in the heavens will be shaken.

"And then they will see 'the Son of Man coming in the clouds' with great power and glory, and then he will send out the angels and gather his elect from the four winds, from the end of the earth to the end of the sky.

"Learn a lesson from the fig tree. When its branch becomes tender and sprouts leaves, you know that summer is near. In the same way, when you see these things happening, know that he is near, at the gates. Amen, I say to you, this generation will not pass away until all these things have taken place. Heaven and earth will pass away, but my words will not pass away.

"But of that day or hour, no one knows, neither the angels in heaven, nor the Son, but only the Father."

Meditation (*Meditatio*)

After the reading, take some time to reflect in silence on one or more of the following questions:

- What word or words in this passage caught your attention?
- What in this passage comforted you?
- What in this passage challenged you?

If practicing lectio divina *as a family or in a group, after the reflection time, invite the participants to share their responses.*

Prayer (*Oratio*)

Read the scripture passage one more time. Bring to the Lord the praise, petition, or thanksgiving that the Word inspires in you.

Contemplation (*Contemplatio*)

Read the Scripture again, followed by this reflection:

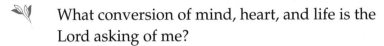 What conversion of mind, heart, and life is the Lord asking of me?

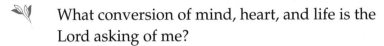 *They will see "the Son of Man coming in the clouds" with great power and glory.* When have I become aware of God's power and glory? How can I be more aware of God's presence?

 Learn a lesson from the fig tree. What lessons do I need learn to be more faithful? What resources do I have to grow in faith?

Heaven and earth will pass away, but my words will not pass away. What passing things do I rely on? How can I grow in my reliance on God's holy Word?

After a period of silent reflection and/or discussion, all recite the Lord's Prayer and the following:

Closing Prayer

O Lord, my allotted portion and my cup,
　　you it is who hold fast my lot.
I set the Lord ever before me;
　　with him at my right hand I shall not be disturbed.

Therefore my heart is glad and my soul rejoices,
　　my body, too, abides in confidence;
because you will not abandon my soul to the netherworld,
　　nor will you suffer your faithful one to undergo
　　　　corruption.

You will show me the path to life,
　　fullness of joys in your presence,
　　the delights at your right hand forever.

From Psalm 16

Living the Word This Week

How can I make my life a gift for others in charity?

Join a Catholic bible study in your parish or online.

November 21, 2021

Lectio Divina for the Solemnity of Our Lord Jesus Christ, King of the Universe

We begin our prayer:
In the name of the Father, and of the Son, and of the Holy Spirit. Amen.

Almighty ever-living God,
whose will is to restore all things
in your beloved Son, the King of the universe,
grant, we pray,
that the whole creation, set free from slavery,
may render your majesty service
and ceaselessly proclaim your praise.
Through our Lord Jesus Christ, your Son,
who lives and reigns with you in the unity of the Holy Spirit,
one God, for ever and ever.

Collect, Solemnity of Our Lord Jesus Christ, King of the Universe

Reading (*Lectio*)

Read the following Scripture two or three times.

John 18:33b-37

Pilate said to Jesus, "Are you the King of the Jews?"
Jesus answered, "Do you say this on your own
or have others told you about me?" Pilate answered,
"I am not a Jew, am I? Your own nation and the chief

priests handed you over to me. What have you done?" Jesus answered, "My kingdom does not belong to this world. If my kingdom did belong to this world, my attendants would be fighting to keep me from being handed over to the Jews. But as it is, my kingdom is not here." So Pilate said to him, "Then you are a king?" Jesus answered, "You say I am a king. For this I was born and for this I came into the world, to testify to the truth. Everyone who belongs to the truth listens to my voice."

Meditation (*Meditatio*)

After the reading, take some time to reflect in silence on one or more of the following questions:

- What word or words in this passage caught your attention?
- What in this passage comforted you?
- What in this passage challenged you?

If practicing lectio divina *as a family or in a group, after the reflection time, invite the participants to share their responses.*

Prayer (*Oratio*)

Read the scripture passage one more time. Bring to the Lord the praise, petition, or thanksgiving that the Word inspires in you.

Contemplation (*Contemplatio*)

Read the Scripture again, followed by this reflection:

What conversion of mind, heart, and life is the Lord asking of me?

Do you say this on your own or have others told you about me? What do I say about Jesus? How do I speak to others about my faith?

My kingdom does not belong to this world. Which of my values reflect the values of the world? What can I do to change them?

Everyone who belongs to the truth listens to my voice. How do I hear God's voice? How can I be more receptive to God's truth?

After a period of silent reflection and/or discussion, all recite the Lord's Prayer and the following:

Closing Prayer

The Lord is king, in splendor robed;
    robed is the Lord and girt about with strength.

And he has made the world firm,
    not to be moved.
Your throne stands firm from of old;
    from everlasting you are, O Lord.

Your decrees are worthy of trust indeed;
    holiness befits your house,
    O Lord, for length of days.

From Psalm 93

Living the Word This Week

How can I make my life a gift for others in charity?

Reflect on the relationship between charity and truth in Pope Benedict's encyclical, *Caritatis in Veritate: http://www.vatican. va/content/benedict-xvi/en/encyclicals/documents/hf_ben-xvi_ enc_20090629_caritas-in-veritate.html.*